AF703239

A Decentralized Technology Model Incorporating Reinforcement Learning for Protected and Energy-Conserving Infrastructures

Custos Veritatis Leo

A Decentralized Technology Model Incorporating Reinforcement Learning for Protected and Energy-Conserving Infrastructures

First Edition March 2025

Written by Custos Veritatis Leo

Contents

Chapter 1

Introduction

In Wireless Sensor Networks, nodes are deployed randomly throughout the network and these nodes work without human intervention. Sensor devices can be monitored remotely by authorized persons only but sometimes hackers attack to destroy or steal data from the network. Sensor nodes are connected in such a way that they can broadcast data in the network according to the routing algorithm in an appropriate manner. WSN itself has many limitations such as sensor devices present in the network having less storage capacity and low battery backup.

Security and power constraints are the main concerns in wireless sensor networks. Sensor nodes can be deployed in inaccessible areas to study its various factors. WSNs are widely used systems throughout the world nowadays. For instance, notable WSN applications are military, healthcare, environmental, traffic control, education, and home care. In healthcare, nodes are deployed on the body of the patient so that a doctor can monitor and diagnose the illness. The defense forces utilize sensor devices to control and monitor the suspected activities in the territory. In WSNs, data nodes themselves are the routers where transmission is done in multi-hops to reach the data packet to its final destination and these sensor nodes carry vulnerable data that can be attacked and destroyed by the wrongdoers. Data transmitted by the sensor nodes is all in the air and prone to attacks. Furthermore, sensor nodes can fail at any point of transmission in the network because of their low energy constraint.

WSN is formed by deploying sensor nodes in either a structured or unstructured manner to get the data from locations where the presence of humans is not necessary. There can be many sensor nodes in a network and these nodes transmit data directly to the sink nodes or the base stations. Sometimes the nodes in WSNs transmit the sensitive data from one place to another, any attack or malicious activity in the network leads to the wrong decision making which can affect major organisational strategies. Sensors can be either mobile nodes or static nodes as per the needs of the user.

In Figure 1.1, ordinary nodes provide data to cluster heads, and the cluster heads then send the data to base stations. Additionally, wireless sensors are linked to the internet, allowing end users to view and use the data for a variety of purposes. The effective data flow from individual nodes to the larger network is ensured by this hierarchical structure, which makes connectivity and information dissemination possible.

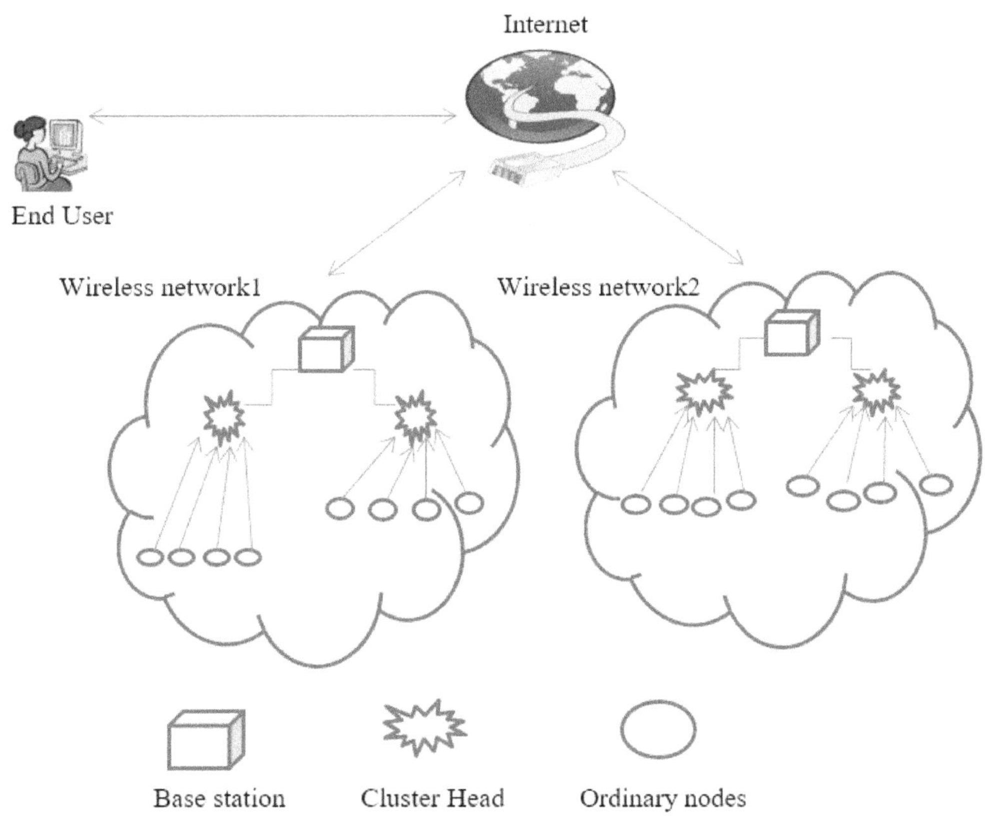

Figure 1.1: WSN Architecture

There are five units in a sensor node:

• **Power Unit:** It is the energy source of the node that provides power backup to the device to perform the required task.

• **Memory Unit:** It stores the data collected from the sensing unit to send it to the base station.

• **Processing Unit:** It performs essential calculations on collected data before sending it to the base station or sink node.

• **Sensing Unit:** It is the most significant unit of the WSN device as it senses the data from the environment without any human intervention. It also converts the continuous data into digital form.

• **Transceiver:** It transmits and receives the collected data.
Apart from this, additional components can be deployed like a location finder, energy generator, mobilizer, etc. in a sensor node.

1.1 Attacks in WSN:

Attacks in WSN can be categorized into two modules:

1.1.1 Active Attacks

Wireless Sensor Networks (WSNs) are vulnerable to many kinds of attacks because of their intrinsic features, like their distributed nature, resource limitations, and wireless connectivity. In this, attackers try to alter or steal the data that is transmitted by the sensors in the network. Cyber attackers can introduce malicious data or nodes into the network, thereby disrupting the normal operations and transmission processes of the system. Table 1.1 shows various types of active attacks:

Table 1.1: Active Attacks

Sr. no.	Attack	Layer
1	Jamming	Physical Layer
2	Tampering	
3	Exhaustion	Data Link Layer
4	Collision	
5	Sybil attack	Network Layer
6	Selective Forwarding	
7	Sinkhole	
8	Wormhole	
9	Black hole	
10	Hello Flooding	
11	Flooding	Transport Layer
12	Clone attack	Application Layer

1.1.2 Passive Attacks

Passive attacks in Wireless Sensor Networks involve unauthorized monitoring or interception of communication without altering the transmitted data. In this, hackers or attackers do not directly attack data to steal or change the information. However, they can listen and analyze the data exchanged by the nodes. These attacks are not easy to detect because attackers just gain confidential knowledge of the data and network to further use it to perform active attacks. Example- Eavesdropping.

1.2 Blockchain

Blockchain emerged as the most secure solution for exchanging transactions in this era of the Internet. This is in sharp contrast to existing technologies, which require trust to be established through middlemen, blockchain is different as it is decentralized and one can send or receive valuable assets directly without involving a third party. Blockchain-based networks are open, tamper-proof, and provide information storage and sharing facilities.

Blockchain is an open ledger that may effectively record business transactions between two parties in a way that is both verifiable and permanent. Within the realm of commerce, this refers to people making purchases or businesses that buy and sell in actual physical locations. Customers usually receive a receipt for their purchases from stores, and the banking database keeps a record of the transaction. Banks keep track of monthly expenses, account balances, and incoming funds in a ledger. The challenge lies in the centralization of banks within each country, necessitating trust in these institutions to safeguard our money. The potential vulnerability arises when considering the possibility of a disruption in the banking system, leading to concerns about the safety of our accounts. Despite these concerns, a level of trust in these centralized authorities remains a requisite.

To prevent problems Blockchain is utilized. Blockchain is an open ledger which means there's no central point. Everyone can participate in the community and a ledger is a place where records are being written. In blockchain, every transaction is permanent and no one can alter or steal the data. For eg. - if two individuals A and B are there, and A wants to sell a watch, then that transaction is irreversible because the idea is if A gives the watch to B, B gives money to A then this is irreversible. Since A will not get his watch back unless a new transaction is made like if A purchases the watch back from B then this trade can be reversed so it is permanent.

The block is only a container for data. Each block contains various important things: data, hash, and hash of the previous block. Information may be anything for e.g. – Data of Bitcoin including transactions. In the file storage block, it contains the filename, size, and date. Every block contains a hash as well, which serves as a distinct fingerprint that uniquely identifies the block. To get this identification, every piece of data that is stored in a block is run through a hash function, which produces a unique code. Interestingly, if you change anything in the block, even a single character, the hash of the block gets completely changed. Furthermore, each block includes the hash of the preceding block, establishing a chain of blocks. In this sequential arrangement, each block points to the one that precedes it in the list, creating the fundamental structure of a blockchain.

To prevent this cube out of hackers there are two security mechanisms in a blockchain i.e. Consensus algorithm and P2P network. Blockchain uses the SHA256 hashing algorithm to save its data from hackers. Other than information, a block consists of the hash value, the previous block's hash, block number, timestamp, and a nonce. A fault-tolerant method to attain a general agreement by following the predefined set of rules between two parties is called a consensus mechanism. The major issue in a decentralized peer-to-peer network is to gain the confidence of all the network nodes in the presence of harmful nodes in the network. In the case of Blockchain technology, 51% of the present network nodes need to be agreed according to the contract to achieve the consensus. The consensus algorithm develops based on the agreement through which every network node reaches a common consensus to add a block to the Blockchain. This builds trust between nodes of the network and provides better reliability. Verification of a block to be added on Blockchain, whether this block is validated by a miner and a copy is scattered among all participant nodes, is done by the Consensus mechanism. An algorithm to reach a consensus is a must to follow Blockchain protocol. Validators or miners are responsible for kicking the faulty nodes out of the network. There are numerous Blockchain platforms available in the market today however Bitcoin, Ethereum, and Hyper Fabric are most popular among all. The pivotal characteristics of a Blockchain are –

I. Peer-to-peer network

II. Reliability

II. Scalability

The consensus mechanism of a Blockchain mostly depends upon the above three features. The majority of consensus mechanisms allow only those users to append a block in the chain that shares some assets or indulges them seriously in the process so that only genuine participants in the network perform duties reliably.

1.2.1 WSN and Blockchain

Security is the most important issue in a centralized wireless network. To tackle this obstacle, blockchain is integrated with a wireless sensor network, thus making this network decentralized. This decreases the overhead of maintaining large databases because the whole data is scattered over the network. Moreover, it consumes less energy comparatively. Blockchain eliminates the server-client centralized network by replacing it with a peer-to-peer network that provides numerous advantages while dealing with sensitive information. Figure 1.2, shows that Wireless Sensor Networks utilize internal blockchains to transmit data and a global blockchain can be created by combining two or more internal blockchains.

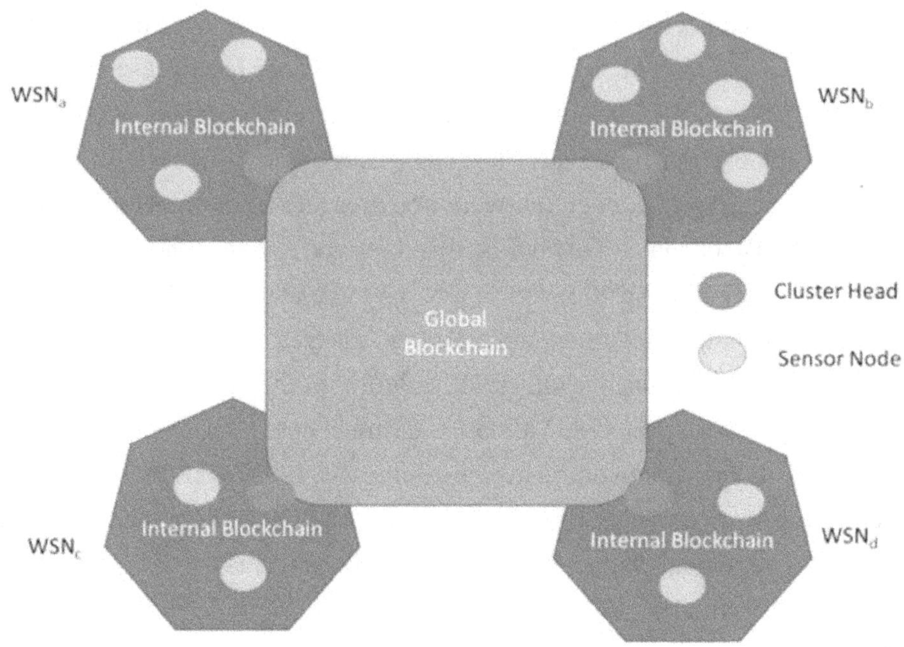

Figure 1.2: Blockchain Employed WSN model

WSN- With and without Blockchain:
Nowadays, the number of devices participating in networks is burgeoning, and data between these nodes is being transmitted by using a central authority in a centralized network. This approach doesn't seem to be effective because nodes in the network are exceedingly high in numbers. Therefore, integrating blockchain technology with WSN will resolve various problems of a centralized network. Blockchain can easily handle a large number of devices in WSN. The WSN system handles the connection between various sensing devices whereas blockchain provides security and reliability to the network. Blockchain doesn't use any central authority to transmit and receive data because it uses distributed techniques to commit transactions thus defends data tampering.

In a centralized system, as shown in Figure 1.3, sensors transmit the sensed data to routers through the network, and then this data reaches the central server through

Figure 1.3: Data Flow in WSN through Centralized Server.

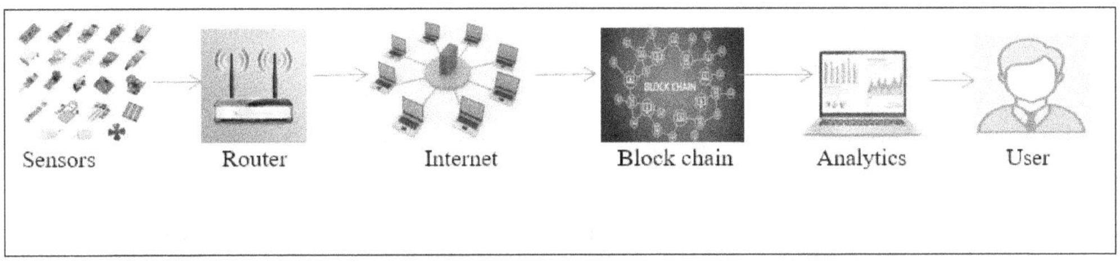

Figure 1.4: Data Flow in WSN through Blockchain Network.

the internet. In the end, the user receives data after analysis. In this user has to rely on central authority which is prone to hacks.

In a Blockchain system, as shown in Figure 1.4, sensor nodes send the data to the internet through a network by using routers, and afterward, data is put into a blockchain instead of the server. The user receives the data after analysis. In this, the end user directly gets the data from the distributed blockchain.

1.2.2 Pros of using Blockchain in WSN

• Cost effective

Blockchain need not to maintain hefty servers because it distributes the processing requirements and data is stored on all nodes present in the network. Today, blockchain is among the favorite technologies to use in various fields like real estate, e-commerce, medical, education, logistics, etc. Blockchain plays an important role in making transactions safe, quicker, and transparent. Moreover, it reduces the transaction cost because users need not pay anything to middlemen. One can trace his transaction easily as blockchain is based on distributed model so every deal reflects on all the devices present in the network. Furthermore, blockchain reduces regulatory fines, operating expenses, and fraud expenses that usually happen in centralized banks [79].

- **Decentralization**

Blockchain provides a decentralized solution for both transaction and communication. It is managed and handled by all the participants of the network rather than a single centralized server. Nodes present in the network make the decisions to commit any transaction according to mutual consensus. If 51% nodes of the network agree to commit a transaction, only then a new block, that contains the required deal, is added to the chain. So, integration of blockchain with WSN results in better efficiency and transparency.

- **Security**

Block in a blockchain consists of the hash value of the previous block, timestamp, nonce, and the data of the transaction. Merkel tree is used to calculate the hash function employed in the system which makes it difficult to modify the data. As shown in Figure 1.5, the block of a blockchain contains two parts, one is the blockchain header and another one is the blockchain body. In the header of the blockchain, there is a block number, hash of the previous block, transaction data, nonce, hash of current block with time stamp, and Merkel tree. A timestamp is a digital postmark that cannot be changed. Every transaction in the blockchain is time-stamped which gives accurate proof of the time at which the transaction is created and it is a pivotal securities add-on in this mechanism [62]. Blockchain doesn't contain the real information rather it consists of the hash values after encoding the original data. This hash (SHA256) function is only one-way and cannot reversed back once encoded.

- **Reliability**

Cloud servers or base stations identify and authenticate the data in WSNs to perform processing and storage activities. Each node in the Wireless sensor network is vulnerable to attacks and its data can be used illegally. When blockchain gets integrated into the WSN, it provides high security and reliability to the system. According to this, data can be used by only participating nodes in a particular transaction. Blockchain can easily recover a dead node by writing a node recovery smart contract. So, using blockchain in WSN provides better security and reliability to the users [11].

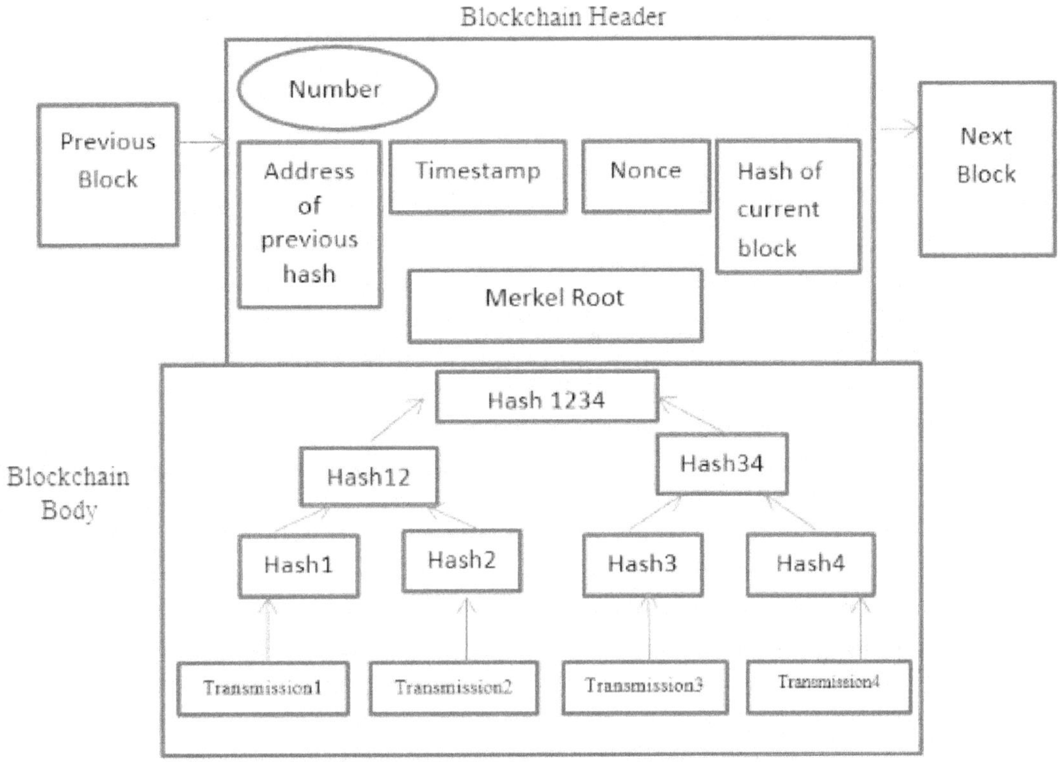

Figure 1.5: Blockchain Structure.

• Temper proof

Blockchain is a growing chain in which new transactions are added in the form of blocks and each block is linked with each other by containing the address of the previous hash in the header. The first block of the chain is called the genesis block. There are many consensus mechanisms available today through which decisions can be easily made for when and which block is added to the chain [167].

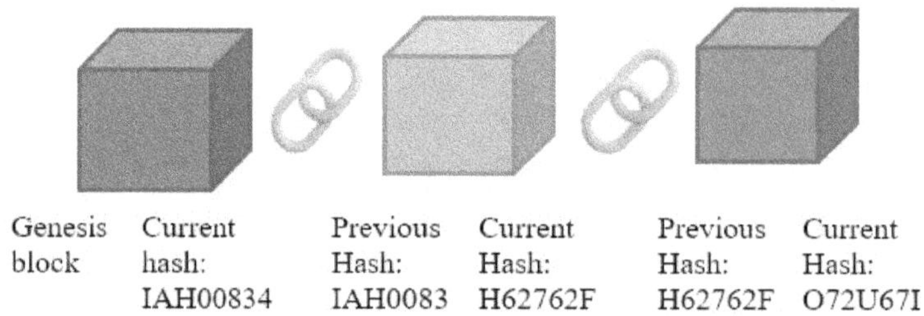

Figure 1.6: Tamper-Proof Block Structure.

Figure 1.6, clearly shows that every data in the blockchain is trackable and cannot be tampered with, as every block contains the address of the previous hash. If someone tries to change the transaction data then the hash value of the block gets changed which again is associated with the previous hash so the hash of that block will also change, similarly all the previous blocks need to get a new hash that is impossible.

• Transparency

One of the most important features of blockchain technology is transparency. Each transaction of the blockchain network is scattered over the network i.e. a copy of the transaction is sent to all the nodes present in the network so whenever a malicious node tries to tamper with the data of the transaction, it needs to modify that data on all other nodes in the completely impossible network. A node needs the control of a minimum of 51% of nodes of the network to make any changes in the transaction.

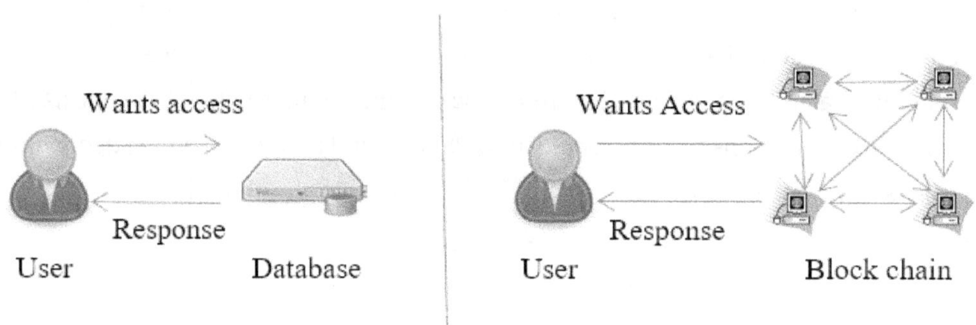

Figure 1.7: Centralized Model vs Blockchain-based Model.

In Figure 1.7, when a user needs access in the centralized model, it directly gets access from the database, on the other hand, in the Blockchain-based model, when the user requests access, it gives the response after scattering that information in the network.

• Immutability

It means to preserve data forever. Once a block is added to the blockchain; it will never be changed or lost. This is the most interesting feature of the blockchain. Immutability is achieved by combining cryptography and hashing techniques because the SHA256 algorithm cannot be reverse-engineered. Hence the data entered in the blockchain is permanent whether it is true or false; it cannot be altered or deleted and no one can delete the history of the blockchain ledger. The block header contains the hashes of the Merkle tree and other previous blocks. If an invader is present in the network, it will degrade the overall performance of the network. A malicious node in the network, that can tamper with the data, can be identified with the help of the response time of the transaction, delayed transmission of data, and forwarding rate of the data [16].

1.2.3 Cons of using Blockchain in WSN

• Storage

In WSNs, the Sink node is considered as a storage node. All the sensor nodes sense the data and send it to the sink node hence, the sink node consumes a lot of energy so it sometimes blocks the network and becomes a dead node. There are three types of storage in WSN: Local storage, External storage, and Data-centric storage [140]. Every transaction in the blockchain is stored in a block and reflected on each device present in the network. Blocks of transactions are increasing on a large scale every day so every node's storage is also getting filled whenever a block is added to the chain. Storage of wireless sensor nodes is limited which is why deploying a blockchain on Wireless sensor networks is not an easy task.

• Difficult to implement and maintain

Blockchain-skilled developers are still fewer in numbers which is why implementing and maintaining this technology is challenging for companies. Although many platforms of blockchain are easily available yet industrialists need to spend a lot of money to work with this new technology. Experts charge a hefty amount to maintain the working of this technology. Traditional developers are not very aware of this technology so one needs to start from scratch in order to become a blockchain developer.

• **Consumes high power**

As already discussed the whole data on the blockchain network is scattered over the network and a copy is maintained by all the nodes participating in the Wireless network. The wireless sensors consume a lot of energy during data transmission resulting in dead nodes many times. Moreover, hashing and encryption are two pillars of blockchain technology, and both of these increase the consumption of energy. The number of nodes in the network and the distance of nodes from one another also affect the node's energy [44]. Data is sensed by the sensors and collected at a midway node which is called the sink node or base station. These nodes have limited memory, less energy, and less processing power and they need transceivers, microcontrollers, and batteries.

• **Scalability**

Scalability is the prime issue while using blockchain with WSN. The usage of blockchain is escalating day by day, whenever a transaction is completed, a block needs to be added to the chain and this chain becomes longer. This does not affect only the software of the system rather it risks hardware failure too. Moreover, the block size of the blockchain is also increasing; initially, the size of the block was around 1Mb. The number of transactions is rising day by day so the size of the block is also expanding. Another issue raised due to scalability is response time, each transaction needs to go through the validation process, and since the number of transactions is growing every moment they have to wait in a queue for validation.

• **Low processing speed**

In blockchain-based wireless sensor networks, many duplicate smart contracts are embedded in blocks. The number of identical smart contracts increases with the increment of load in the network which results in wastage of memory as well as lowers the processing speed of network [89]. WSNs usually are heterogeneous and contain

1000s of low-processing sensor nodes in them.

• Legal difficulties

Blockchain is a decentralized technology, so numerous users (nodes) from all over the world can become members of blockchain. Every country and region has different rules and regulations that may not apply to the blockchain system. The law of every government works according to the written or verbal constitution of that region, which is why it is more difficult to specify whether a fraudulent transaction in the blockchain is legal or not in that particular region. Moreover, this technology is prone to cyber-attacks.

1.2.4 Common Factors for all the Blockchains

• Decentralized

The most phenomenal attribute of blockchain is that the network is decentralized and no trusted third party is needed to make transactions.

• Cryptography

Everyone wants to be sure that their valuables are properly protected with the help of the best available algorithms. Blockchain uses two types of cryptographic algorithms, asymmetric-key algorithms, and hash functions. Blockchain provides the ability to adjust the encryption algorithms according to the needs which facilitates the user to work easily.

• Distributed

A blockchain is distributed over several machines in real-time. A copy of the record is updated on each computer after every transaction and this abolishes the need for mediators.

• Time stamped

Every record on the blockchain can be traced and verified easily because these all transactions are time-stamped.

• Programmable

Instructions of blocks enable any actions to be performed if certain conditions are met and it cannot be accompanied by digital data.

• Digital Signatures

It mainly consists of two parts: the signature algorithm and the verification algorithm. The signature algorithm is to generate the digital signatures and the verification algorithm is to verify the signatures of the message.

• Consensus mechanism

It is used to determine the accounting of nodes in the blockchain-based network and also used to verify the information on record. There are many workable consensus mechanisms nowadays i.e. PoW, PoA, PoS.

1.3 Consensus Mechanisms

• Proof of Work (PoW)

The most preferred and simplest mechanism that was used in Bitcoin, the first application of this type, is Proof of Work. This mechanism reveals the miner who will add the next block in the chain. This algorithm is based on a mathematical calculation to crack an equation to find a required number; the node that solves this riddle earliest will win and become the next miner. Though the algorithm is manageable yet a lot of energy is consumed while solving the arithmetic equation. The whole process of solving the puzzle and adding a block to a chain is known as mining. Most of the time, miners took many transactions together in a block and tried to mine it. Miners need to solve the problem to achieve the target hash. It becomes more complicated to mine a block if the target number is low and whoever mines the block gets a reward in return. It consumes a lot of time and energy of miners; hence they need to check different nonce values to solve the puzzle. Despite this, the cost of mining is much higher because of numerous electricity and special hardware i.e. graphic card needed to complete the process.

• Proof of Stake (PoS)

The most suitable alternative to the Proof of Work algorithm is Proof of Stake. Miners in PoW are called validators in PoS. In this mechanism, the node that has more stake value has more chances to get the opportunity to become a validator. However, it doesn't give any guarantee to be a validator for the biggest stakeholder rather it follows a randomized process to find a validator with high chances for a node with maximum stake. Users need to put some amount of cryptocurrency as a debt to become validators and can lose that money if it plays unfairly. The validator has to create and append a block in the chain rather than waste its energy by doing unnecessary computation as in PoW. If a faulty user wants to alter the block in the chain by becoming a validator, it needs to have 51% stake and it's unsafe for the malicious node because whenever it attests to a false node it risks losing its stake. In this mechanism, electricity usage is much lower than PoW and no special equipment is required hence it is an energy-efficient algorithm.

• **Proof of Authority (PoA)**

PoW and PoS work in a permissionless network whereas PoA is designed to work in a permissioned network. Every node available in the network is first authorized and then let it to enter the network. According to the algorithm, nodes, that are reputed and successfully validated blocks in the past, or preapproved, are likely to be validators. PoA's performance is much better than that of PoW and PoS, which is why it is suitable for private blockchains. It's not an easy task to become a validator in PoA, it follows a robust process and one needs to put its reputation at stake and invest more money. Just like PoW and PoS, the hacker needs to get control of 51% of nodes to commit any faulty activity in PoA, hence it is a permissioned network, and controlling 51% pre-authenticated nodes is an impossible task. Comparatively, a few numbers of validators are there in PoA and it consumes less power and resources during validation.

• **Proof of Capacity (PoC)**

In this mechanism, miners utilize the memory of the computer system rather than using computational power as in PoW. Node needs to provide its hardware space to the network so that it can store solutions to hashing issues. Node, which can assign larger storage units to the network, will store more hashing solutions hence getting more chances to become a miner. It doesn't mean if a node constitutes itself in mining activity through PoC can never use that space for other business, rather it can wipe off the mining data anytime from its computer and utilize that space for any other project. PoW takes 10 minutes to create a block whereas PoC takes only 4 minutes. Blockchains that run on proof of capacity include Storj, Burst, Chia, and SpaceMint.

• **Proof of Burn (PoB)**
The most common alternative to the Proof of Work algorithm is Proof of Burn because it consumes minimal energy as compared to the former one. In PoB, the system doesn't need any super gadget to solve the mathematical problem rather it burns crypto as an investment in the blockchain system, so by consuming these coins just for investment sake, users could not take risks to validate invalid transactions. The more investment a user makes, the more the chances a node gets to become a validator because it gets more power to mine a block. The difference between PoS and PoB is that in PoS, a user can withdraw anytime from the system and get their money back but in PoB, the user has to destroy the coins forever to gain profit.

• **Proof of Elapsed time (PoET)**
In Proof of Elapsed Time, nodes get a certain amount of time that is randomly decided by the system. The "miners" must first join the network, gaining a membership certificate. Once they are in the network, the nodes need to wait a certain amount of time which is randomly decided. The miner must wait at least the amount of time that was defined before starting to mine a new block into the blockchain. In PoET, the miner that has the shortest amount of time is elected to do the block mining that round. The system tends to be fair and chooses miners with a good degree of randomness. It doesn't require much electricity consumption and miners can "go to sleep" while they wait for their turn. The PoET algorithm is for permissioned blockchain networks. That is, a special verification is required from a node when it tries to join the network.

1.4 Attacks on Blockchain

Aggarwal *et al.* [2] categorized Blockchain attacks into four modules :
• **Mining Attacks**
• **Network Communication Attacks**

- **Smart Contract based Attacks**
- **Wallet-based Attacks**

1.4.1 Mining Attacks

• 51% Attack

In a 51% attack, an attacker can gain more than 50% control of the mining power in the blockchain network. The term "51%" refers to the threshold at which an attacker controls more computational power than the rest of the honest network combined. With this power, an attacker can create an alternate long chain of blocks and steal the reward from the honest chain. The attacker needs to maintain control over the majority hash power for an extended period to carry out the benefits from the attack.

• Selfish Mining Attack

In a Selfish mining attack, the attacker mines privately but does not broadcast it to the network. The attacker continues to mine on a private chain. Selfish mining attacks try to gain a disproportionate advantage in the mining process by withholding mined blocks. The attacker strategically releases the private chain to the network at a point where it can override the public chain. Once its length surpasses the public chain length, the miner broadcasts it. Selfish mining can disrupt the fairness of mining rewards in the blockchain.

• Block Withholding Attack

In a block withholding attack, the attacker is only required to reasonably allocate the attack computing power. However, the miner who launches a block withholding attack always submits partial proof of work, the pool manager only discovers that it has encountered a block withholding attack but cannot identify the malicious miners in the mining pool. Because the block withholding attack cannot provide any effective help to the attacked mining pool, it even helps the attacker get part of the revenue in the attacked mining pool [35]. Therefore, this attack can cause serious harm to the mining process.

• Longest Chain Attack

In a longest-chain attack, an attacker attempts to create a longer blockchain privately and then releases it to the network to replace the existing honest blockchain. The goal of a longest-chain attack is to create a longer blockchain than the legitimate chain by mining more blocks in private. The attacker can potentially control or manipulate transactions on the blockchain. In this, the attacker assumes that all the nodes present in the network will accept the longer false chain as the valid one.

1.4.2 Network Communication Attacks

• Sybil Attack

In a Sybil attack, a single node within the network falsely presents itself as several different nodes. As shown in Figure 1.8, by creating false identities, the attacker aims to infiltrate the network, establishing connections with legitimate nodes. This infiltration allows the attacker to manipulate the network's routing data, altering it to serve their malicious purposes. The attacker can create an overwhelming number of false nodes, seeking to gain control over the entire network. This control enables them to manipulate the network's operations, leading to data loss and potential harm to the system as a whole. The entire network can be destabilized as the attacker creates numerous fake identities, overshadowing the legitimate nodes and preventing them from effectively transmitting and receiving data.

Researchers have made efforts to detect and counteract Sybil attacks in WSNs. [115] have employed machine learning techniques to identify Sybil attacks in WSNs. [121] have proposed a method that combines CAM-PVM (Compare and Match-Position Verification Method) with MAP (Message Authentication and Passing) to detect and prevent Sybil attacks in WSNs. Despite these efforts, the threat of Sybil attacks continues to loom over WSNs, necessitating further measures to safeguard the networks.

• Eclipse Attack

In an Eclipse attack, an attacker isolates the target node by controlling all its connections in the network so that he can manipulate the target node to provide false data and transactions. The attacker tries to control the information received by the targeted node, potentially leading to various security vulnerabilities. This attack makes a node disoriented so it can make incorrect decisions accepting the fraudulent transaction, breaching the network fairness. Here, the attacker requests a malicious

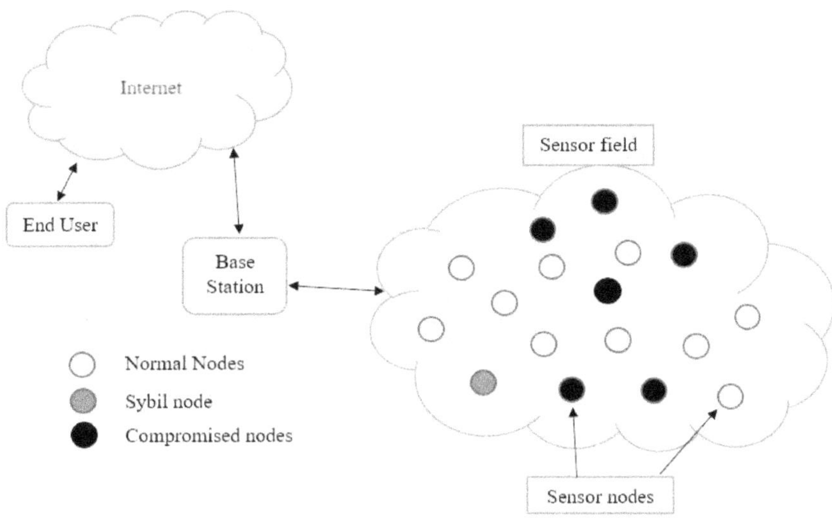

Figure 1.8: Sybil Attack

forced construction link to fill the routing table of the victim node before restarting the victim node in the blockchain such that the victim node is forced to establish a routing connection with the attacker after restarting. Then, the attacker establishes incoming connection requests to the victim miner node constantly to monopolize the victim node channel and control its information flow. As a result, attacked miner nodes are forced to receive and forward the error or malicious blockchain ledger information sent by the attackers [41]. It involves financial losses that's why it categorizes as a most phenomenal attack for blockchain.

• **DDoS Attack**

In a Distributed Denial of Service (DDoS) attack, a malicious node attempts to interrupt the network so that it cannot operate properly by flooding a massive volume of traffic on the network. DDoS attacks do not just spoil the blockchain networks, but they influence blockchain networks and related services, resulting in congestion, delays in transaction processing, and inaccessibility in immoderate cases hence degrading the overall performance of the network. If a significant number of nodes are affected, the overall resilience and performance of the blockchain may suffer. More decentralized blockchain networks may be more resilient to DDoS attacks since there is no central point of failure.

1.4.3 Smart Contract-based Attacks

• Proxy Call Attack

A proxy call attack is an attack that makes smart contracts insecure and influences the performance of the blockchain network. In this, the attacker tries to spoil the development, design, and implementation of a smart contract proxy that allows them to alter the behavior of the contract or steal sensitive information. Proxy contracts are frequently used in upgradable contracts in which the logic of the contract can be updated by not modifying the address of the contract. In this, an attacker creates malicious data or parameters so that it can execute unintentional code while implementing smart contracts.

• Information Leakage Attack

In this, users can transmit their transactions on the blockchain network; however, all the transactions are propagated to all the nodes present in the network. In this, smart contracts involve unauthorized disclosure or exposure of sensitive information stored within the contract. It is not feasible to store sensitive information or credentials on the smart contracts. [35] involves four methods for this attack: 1) The attacker obtains a list of servers using a message query. 2) Based on the address information in the network and the list of servers, the attacker creates an anonymous list comprising attack targets. 3) The attacker uses other nodes to uniquely identify the client (i.e., network address translation or peer behind a firewall) in the anonymized list. 4) The attacker monitors the transaction information sent by the client using other nodes and obtains the relevant information of the transaction sender based on the data transmitted by the client.

• Reentrancy

One of the most lethal attacks in smart contracts is the Reentrancy attack. In this, the attacker withdraws someone else's capital by again and again calling the target's withdraw function. When the smart contract falls short of amending the victim's balance, before transferring funds, the attacker can continuously call the withdraw function to drain the contract's funds [150]. One of the most significant hacks in the history of crypto, the DAO hack, in which 60 million dollars of ethers were stolen, is a well-known real-world reentrancy attack.

• Smart Contract Overflow and Underflow

An overflow error attack on a smart contract occurs when more value is provided than the maximum value. Whenever this occurs, it revolves back to zero and this increasing of value again and again can spoil the network. Underflow attack is the exact converse of the overflow error. In this, despite providing more value, the system surpasses the minimum value, triggering an increase towards the maximum value instead of reverting to zero. If a program lacks the feature that checks for underflow and overflow, an attacker can get more tokens than they own. They can also get a maxed-out balance, which is essentially stealing. Furthermore, these attacks can cause the whole system to break because the amount of tokens being maxed out is not the same as the number of tokens in the system.

1.4.4 Wallet-based Attacks

• Double Spending

A double-spending attack refers to a different number of transactions occurring where the cryptocurrencies are the same. In this, the user first signs off and requests a transaction through their user wallet. This unconfirmed transaction takes place in a pool of unconfirmed transactions, from where the miner picks transactions and solves complicated mathematical problems through PoW consensus to get hash output as a unique one and broadcast them to add the block to the blockchain. If other miners verify these hashes, only then, the block will be added. Then, the corrupted miner picks transactions and adds blocks to the isolated chain by verifying them with strong computational power faster than the good miners who add blocks to the real blockchain. The corrupted miner broadcasts the isolated blockchain's transaction to the real blockchain when the isolated chain is larger than the real one and the miner of the real chain tries to add their block to the isolated one. The democratic governance rule states that the blocks will add to the larger one by removing the previous records that they have. The real blockchain's block had the information about the transaction where the corrupted miner spent his currency but the isolated one didn't know about the transaction. So, when the blocks try to add the isolated chain then they would remove the previous transaction information. So, in the new isolated chain, the corrupted miner would be able to spend all of the currencies that he had spent once in the real blockchain [146].

• Crypto-jacking Attack

Crypto-jacking is a type of resource embezzlement attack, wherein an attacker secretly executes the cryptocurrency mining program in the target host to gain profits. In blockchain wallets, a crypto-jacking attack could involve exploiting vulnerabilities in the wallet software or a user's device to use its computational power for mining cryptocurrency. Malicious code is to be written into the wallet's software, either by injecting through software downloads or harmful websites and ads. Honest users do not know about the malevolent websites or ads and they unknowingly click on the scripts that are designed to steal the device's power for illegal mining.

• Wallet Theft

Wallet theft means the unapproved access and control of crypto-currency of a user's wallet by wrongdoers. Blockchain wallets keep private keys that permit access to the user's assets, and assuming these private keys are compromised, it results in the theft of the related digital currency. Preventing such attacks requires the use of intricate and unique passwords that are not easily guessable by potential criminals.

1.5 Blockchain Empowers WSN Security

• Blockchain provides information integrity using a proof of trust.

• Blockchain eases "decentralized consensus" by being a distributed ledger, that is intrinsically resistant to modification of the underlying information, therefore it is tamper-resistant.

• The blockchain intrinsically provides accessibility, openness, incorruptibility, and the ability to store and transfer information in a safe method.

• A blockchain can encourage a wide selection of tasks and trustworthy contracts, that is keeping money safely, all without the intervention of an intermediary.

• A blockchain is an "open stage", it records the transactions on a large number of distributed hosts, provided that a duplicated, decentralized database effectively gets rid of the possibility of international data corruption (deliberate or accidental).

• The blockchain is a database that keeps the complete history of transactions on the system that has its own copy of consensus formation along with the database algorithms to stay synchronized.

• The blockchain incorporates the hash of the block and the hash of the previous block to form a chain.

• Blockchain includes nodes' anonymous entities (processes, people, or consumers) when nodes create transactions, nodes sign these transactions to show that they are the owners of the asset being transferred in the network.

• As consensus algorithms, a P2P system is required to make sure replications across nodes are all undertaken. Peers support the condition of the distributed ledger.

• The blockchain nodes could be block signers or miners. Miners create blocks that contain new relevant data (to be protected). Block signers validate and sign the transaction.

• In blockchain, to find out which node can append the next block, this decision is made using a consensus mechanism.

• Some transaction validation may occur with tokens or some baseline user standing and known algorithms, the data held on a blockchain is a shared database that is consistently and automatically reconciled.

• The database isn't domiciled or saved on a single device or any server, and as a result, the records it embodies are public and verifiable.

1.6 Overview of Reinforcement Learning

The process of converting raw data into information with the help of computers is the core task of computer science. Traditionally, programs were developed by people where every program has one or a set of problems to address. Nowadays, a pivotal concern is to solve these types of problems with the help of artificial intelligence (AI) which has better techniques to develop a program [70].

The main objective of AI is to sort out the problems that are difficult to solve efficiently with the human mind because a specific type of intelligence is needed to solve those issues. Initially, machine learning was developed as a part of AI and it proved as a pivotal technology to resolve the difficulties. Subsequently, a new mechanism, Deep learning was developed to figure out the troubles.

Reinforcement learning through machine learning is the newest technique and a sub-branch of AI. In this, the system learns from itself to make further decisions to riddle out the complications. RL techniques follow the Markov Decisions Process (MDP) which contains environment and agents [10]. In this, an agent makes an effort to accomplish the task by taking relevant steps and coming up with necessary feedback (reward or punishment) to refine the results. RL techniques don't need any advanced information about the environment and this very feature makes it feasible for blockchain. RL technique is classified into two parts, i.e. model-based RL and model-free RL. The key difference between model-based and model-free RL is that in model-based RL, the agent uses the existing learned model to complete the task and in model-free RL, the agent uses a new model and learns it according to the situation. When more than one factors influence the results (reward value) then it is more viable to use model-free RL [75].

1.7 Layout of Thesis

A thorough introduction to Wireless Sensor Networks (WSN), Blockchain, and Reinforcement Learning is given in Chapter 1. The chapter goes into more detail about various attacks on blockchain and WSN. The pros and cons of blockchain technology are also discussed, and several consensus mechanisms are examined.

In Chapter 2, a comprehensive review of the literature is conducted on both traditional and current routing approaches within the context of Blockchain-based Wireless Sensor Networks (WSNs). The chapter also addresses the problem definition and outlines the research objectives.

In Chapter 3, issues and challenges with the existing routing models used in Blockchain-based Wireless Sensor Networks (WSNs) are examined. The chapter carefully describes the research gaps that have been found, highlighting areas that need more study and inquiry.

The suggested work's methodology, which includes a thorough description of the chosen approach, is presented in Chapter 4. The chapter continues with a description of the Simulation Environment that includes setup and condition details. It also explores the procedures of Data Collection and Processing, providing insight into the methods used to get and manage information. This chapter also goes into detail on how the Wireless Sensor Network (WSN) is configured.

In Chapter 5, detail is provided on the integration of the generated dataset with blockchain technology. The chapter elucidates the implementation of Proof of Work (PoW) and Proof of Authority (PoA), offering detailed insights into their execution. Furthermore, a thorough analysis of the initial results is conducted within this chapter, providing a deeper understanding of the outcomes derived from the implemented approach.

in detail. This section offers a thorough examination of the approaches and strategies used throughout the training phase, illuminating how Reinforcement Learning is applied to improve the recovered dataset's functionality.

The details of using Reinforcement Learning to train the recovered dataset are explained in Chapter 6. This section thoroughly examines the approaches and strategies used throughout the training phase, illuminating how Reinforcement Learning is applied to improve the recovered dataset's functionality. Afterward, it presents a detailed exposition of the proposed RL-LEACH algorithm. It elaborates the algorithm, offering insights into its design, structure, and functionality. Additionally, the chapter provides a comprehensive overview of the performance metrics utilized, outlining the criteria used to evaluate and measure the effectiveness of the proposed algorithm. Key features of the proposed work are also discussed, highlighting the distinctive elements that contribute to its innovation and efficacy.

In Chapter 7, the results and discussions of the conducted research are thoroughly elaborated. This section provides a thorough study of the results produced by the suggested model. A comparative evaluation is also given, in which the suggested model is contrasted with more modern models. This comparison facilitates a thorough understanding of the performance and significance of the proposed model.

In Chapter 8, the document concludes with a summary and reflection on the key findings and insights derived from the research. The primary contributions, findings, and implications of the study are summarized in the conclusion section. The chapter also explores the future scope of the work, suggesting directions for investigation and growth.

Chapter 2

Literature Review

2.1 Introduction

Wireless Sensor Networks are widely used for various applications such as environmental monitoring, healthcare systems, and industrial automation. To ensure efficient data transmission and network management in Wireless Sensor Networks, routing protocols play a crucial role. One popular routing protocol for WSNs is the Low Energy Adaptive Clustering Hierarchy protocol [82]. LEACH is a clustering-based protocol that aims to optimize energy efficiency in WSNs.

LEACH works by dividing the network into clusters, with each cluster having a designated Cluster Head responsible for coordinating data transmission within the cluster [93]. The clustering approach in WSNs is crucial for optimizing energy efficiency and prolonging the lifetime of the sensor network. Low-Energy Adaptive Clustering Hierarchy is recognized as one of the most famous clustering protocols in WSNs due to its ability to reduce energy consumption. By utilizing a clustering mechanism, LEACH effectively reduces energy consumption [74] [157] and extends the lifetime of the sensor network. The development of a clustering-based hierarchy protocol has significantly improved the energy efficiency in WSNs, ultimately leading to better performance in terms of system lifetime, latency, and application-perceived quality.

However, along with the benefits of WSN routing protocols, ensuring the security and integrity of data transmission in WSNs is also critical. One approach to enhancing the security of WSNs is through the use of blockchain technology [85]

[54]. Blockchain technology provides a decentralized and secure platform for storing and managing data in WSNs. By leveraging blockchain's decentralized and immutable nature, the integrity and confidentiality of data in WSNs can be ensured. Blockchain technology can provide secure and tamper-proof data storage in WSNs by eliminating the need for a central authority. One proposed solution for combining WSN routing protocols with blockchain-based security is the Reinforcement learning-based LEACH protocol. The Reinforcement learning-based LEACH protocol utilizes reinforcement learning techniques to enhance the efficiency of data transmission in WSNs.

It employs a learning algorithm that adapts the routing decisions based on the network's security requirements, ensuring that data is transmitted through secure and reliable paths [80]. This integration of Reinforcement learning-based LEACH protocol with blockchain technology offers a promising solution to the pressing security concerns in WSNs. By incorporating reinforcement learning, the protocol can dynamically adjust its routing decisions to adapt to changing security threats and requirements, enhancing the overall resilience of the network. This adaptability is crucial in today's dynamic and evolving threat landscape, where traditional static security measures may fall short.

Furthermore, the utilization of blockchain technology in WSNs introduces a layer of trust and transparency in data transactions. The transparency and immutability of blockchain technology help in establishing trust among the various entities involved in WSN data transactions. This trust is particularly crucial in healthcare applications, where the integrity and privacy of patient's data are of utmost importance. By integrating blockchain technology into WSNs for healthcare applications, the security and privacy of patients' data can be significantly enhanced, ultimately contributing to improved healthcare delivery and patient outcomes [21]. In conclusion, the combination of WSN routing protocols with blockchain-based security, particularly the Reinforcement learning-based LEACH protocol, presents a promising approach to addressing the security challenges in WSNs.

2.2 Traditional Approaches

2.2.1 LEACH based Routing

This study of the literature primarily addresses hierarchical routing, exploring several approaches within the cluster-based routing protocol. This analysis centers on several methods used to carry out this routing protocol, intending to offer a thorough comprehension of the hierarchical structure and features that come with cluster-based routing. One of the most famous clustering routing protocols of WSN is LEACH (Low Energy Adaptive Clustering Hierarchy). Cluster formation is a necessary step in the LEACH methodology for sensor node arrangement. One sensor node is selected as the leader or cluster head of each cluster, while the other nodes become cluster members or non-cluster heads. The operational workflow is for every single node to gather information from its surroundings and then send this information to the cluster head for that node [180].

• LEACH-C (Centralized Low Energy Adaptive Clustering Hierarchy)
A variation of the LEACH routing protocol, LEACH-C [60] employed the same steady phase and centralized clustering method as LEACH. During this setup phase, every sensor node shares its position data with the sink, enabling the sink to calculate each node's energy and estimate nodes that have less energy than the network's average. To collect data from cluster heads, the sink broadcasts a message. If CH and ID match in the broadcast message, data is sent to the sink; otherwise, the sink enters sleep mode and waits for its turn to come up. The LEACH-C procedure's steady phase is comparable to the LEACH protocol. LEACH-C is managed and controlled by the base station, but it requires GPS devices for accurate location, and it is costly and consumes additional energy in the network with less scalability.

• TEEN (THRESHOLD SENSITIVE ENERGY EFFICIENT SENSOR NETWORK)
This sensor network is reactive and has threshold sensitivity, making it energy efficient [107]. It is suggested that reactive networks, react quickly to abrupt environmental changes. There are two characteristics: Hard Threshold and Soft Threshold. A sensor node will be chosen as a CH in the network if it precisely satisfies the hard

threshold value. The remaining nodes that satisfy the soft threshold value function as cluster member sensor nodes, detecting their surroundings and sending data to the CH. It is comparable to the LEACH approach for choosing the cluster head. Because there are fewer transmissions in the network, this protocol uses less energy.

• M-LEACH (Mobile-based Low Energy Adaptive Clustering Hierarchy)
Similar to the initial LEACH, M-LEACH uses a threshold-based limit recipe; however, unlike LEACH, M-LEACH takes into account the adaptability of different hubs throughout the information exchange stage [83]. The flexible hub's portability is tested because it has the potential to leave the cluster even while it is sending data to a CH. By verifying if a portable hub is still prepared to communicate with CH as indicated by the TDMA plan, M-LEACH handles these kinds of issues. The hub considers itself to be out of range if it misses two sequential TDMA outlines, and the CH removes inaccessible hubs from its part list.

• S-LEACH (Solar Aware Centralized and Distributed based Low Energy Adaptive Clustering Hierarchy)
A variant of LEACH known as Solar Aware Centralized and Distributed based LEACH, or S-LEACH, was presented by the authors in paper [56]. The lifespan of the WSN has been extended by using solar energy. The S-LEACH stretches out both C-LEACH and basic LEACH. A few hubs in S-LEACH were fueled by sun-oriented energy, and these hubs functioned as CH by essentially depending on their position in relation to the sun. The concentrated and fundamental LEACH protocol is related to the solar-powered plane notion. Sun-based mindful combined LEACH: In combined SLEACH, the sink hub will select the CH with the use of improved centrally controlled computation. In S-LEACH, the sink hub is designated as the CH and the sun-powered position works in tandem with the sensor hubs to transmit energy to the hubs with the highest energy. The lifespan of the system increases as a result of the expansion of the sensor system's execution along with the number of solar-aware hubs. The sensor lifespan is extended by the sun duration. When the sun's duration is shorter, the CH assignment takes place. S-distributed LEACH: In sun-powered dispersed LEACH, the sun-orientated hubs are the required picking inclination.

• **EC-LEACH (Enhanced Centralized Low Energy Adaptive Clustering Hierarchy)**

To build clusters, it employs a centralized and multi-hop communication strategy. The first CH is established based on the threshold values of the sensor nodes; the following round's CH is determined by the base station and is based on the threshold values of the first cluster head, the remaining sensor nodes having threshold values, and the second highest threshold value and least distance node. Because protocol cluster heads are dispersed equitably and centrally, the lifetime of the network is extended [129].

• **V-LEACH (Vice Low Energy Adaptive Clustering Hierarchy)**

Authors in [158] presented a novel version of the LEACH protocol that introduces a unique structure within the cluster that consists of vice-CHs, backup nodes that take over as a CH if the primary CH is unavailable, Cluster Heads (CHs), cluster nodes entrusted with collecting environmental data and forwarding it to the CH, and cluster nodes responsible for reliably and impartially transmitting data from cluster members to the Base Station (BS). The presence of a vice-CH in this V-LEACH protocol becomes essential since it may easily assume the CH responsibilities if the primary CH fails, guaranteeing uninterrupted data transfer from the cluster nodes to the BS.

• **F-LEACH (Fixed Number of cluster-based Low Energy Adaptive Clustering Hierarchy)**

The core concept of cluster arrangement in F-LEACH is that it is the beginning of the system arrangement and is settled later, according to authors in [106]. The CH position revolves around hubs within these clusters, which should resemble a LEACH. This process has an advantage over LEACH in that it does not have arrangement faults at the beginning of each and every round, unlike LEACH. Currently, F-LEACH uses centralized cluster development calculation, which is comparable to CLEACH, for the cluster arrangement. A limitation of the F-LEACH protocol is that its settled clusters do not allow for the addition of additional hubs to the system and do not adjust their behavior when a hub leaves the system.

• **K-LEACH (K-medoids-Low Energy Adaptive Clustering Hierarchy)**

Authors of [19] proposed the K-LEACH protocol, which makes use of the K-medoids clustering calculation to obtain highly consistent hub clustering and excellent CH decisions. It is a highly verifiable fact that WSN energy maintenance is typically higher than that which depends on the collection or clustering of communicating hubs followed by receiving hubs for the correspondence setup stage. LEACH-K considers the distance from the cluster center that is the least. As a result, it serves as a model for the hub's selection as a CH (following the second round). LEACH-K is divided into multiple rounds, with cluster arrangement and steady-state stages included in each round.

• L-LEACH (Energy-Balanced Clustering Algorithm based Low Energy Adaptive Clustering Hierarchy Protocol)

Authors in [90] suggested an improved LEACH algorithm called L-LEACH, or energy-balanced clustering calculation. The core concept that underpins the improved routing protocol over the conventional LEACH suggests modifying the energy computation and expediting the CH's choice. The computation carefully considers the remaining energy and the elements of separation, improves Cluster Head decision-making, and facilitates the process by which the non-Cluster Head hub selects the best CH. The results of the experiment indicate that the energy consumption in L-LEACH differs little from that in the basic LEACH computation. The reasons are as follows: every hub is empowered to consume energy in a moderately adjusted manner; the early demise of low-energy hubs is kept at a safe distance; the system's energy distribution is spared; and the amount of information transmission is impressively upgraded. The enhanced calculation selects CH based on remaining energy and the hub organizes data.

• P-LEACH (Performance Based Low Energy Adaptive Clustering Hierarchy)

Authors of paper [34] introduced an additional improved protocol called P-LEACH, which simplifies the process of reconstructing the cluster and makes better decisions about which CH to choose. It also considers the probability choice of energy-aware multipath Routing (EAMR) and incorporates it into the basic LEACH calculation. The simulation results show that P-LEACH has a longer system life than the standard LEACH technique. Additionally, it suggests that P-LEACH has a longer system lifespan than LEACH.

• **W-LEACH (Weighted Low Energy Adaptive Clustering Hierarchy Aggregation)**
W-LEACH, a modified version of the LEACH protocol with a centralized information-collecting approach, was introduced in [61]. W-LEACH follows the structure of the traditional LEACH technique, with two main stages: a setup stage and a continuous state stage. During the setup phase, each sensor node is given a weighted value that is determined by W-LEACH. The computation of weights is used to determine whether active sensors are CHs; a higher weight corresponds to a higher probability of selection. It is important to note that W-LEACH does not consider whether a sensor has previously served as a CH in recent rounds.

• **MOD-LEACH (Modified Low Energy Adaptive Clustering Hierarchy)**
The Modified LEACH routing protocol is another version of the LEACH protocol; it employs high amplifier signals for inter-communication and low amplifier signals for intra-network communication. Energy can be conserved in networks in this way. This improved form of leach CH is based on the residual energy of the cluster head and checks the residual energy in the sensor node to create CH in the cluster, rather than changing it every cycle. By utilizing the same amplifier signal for both communications, MOD-LEACH extends the lifetime of the network and enhances LEACH [169].

• **E-LEACH (Energy based Low Energy Adaptive Clustering Hierarchy)**
The E-LEACH routing protocol, when compared to the LEACH-based routing protocol, primarily improves the CH choice method [78]. The E-LEACH routing protocol is isolated into different rounds, just like the LEACH-based protocol. As a result, each sensor hub in the first round should have an equal chance of becoming the CH for the current cluster. Following the first transmission round, each hub should have a distinct amount of leftover energy. Based on this, the hub with the highest remaining energy could be selected as the cluster's CH, and other hubs within the cluster could be assigned to areas of the cluster where there may be less energy.

• **HT2H-LEACH (Hybrid Threshold Sensitive and Two-level Heterogeneous Low Energy Adaptive Clustering Hierarchy)**

The heterogeneous LEACH and TEEN (Threshold Sensitive Energy Efficient Sensor Network) protocols' features are combined in the HT2HL protocol. Cluster Heads (CHs) are chosen using weighted probability, and the election process is divided into epochs. This strategy addresses LEACH's weaknesses. Notably, if all CHs are located at a significant distance from the Sensor Nodes (SNs), SNs can establish direct communication with the Base Station (BS). Moreover, SNs modify their transmission power according to their separation from the BS and CHs. One important aspect that helps conserve energy by lowering the amount of transmissions is the addition of thresholds. These developments add to the HT2HL protocol's overall efficacy and efficiency.

• TSI-LEACH (Threshold Sensitive Improved Low Energy Adaptive Clustering Hierarchy)

Authors in [122] proposed a modified LEACH namely TSI-LEACH that is based on two metrics: Heterogeneity of nodes and the current energy of the nodes. In this, Cluster heads (CHs) are chosen using a probabilistic method according to the LEACH protocol. Every node in this procedure creates a random number, which it then compares to a preset threshold value. A node is selected as a cluster head only if the number of nodes within a certain distance is greater than a threshold. Multihop packet transmission to the sink node via multiple cluster heads is considered, and the transmission is allowed only if the minimum distance cluster is not zero.

• I-LEACH (Improved Low Energy Adaptive Clustering Hierarchy)

[148] provided details on how an improved version of the LEACH protocol was implemented in the study is carried out. This development is primarily concerned with reducing power consumption, which is accomplished by introducing an improved cluster head election mechanism during data transfer. This invention is specially made to reduce collisions, guaranteeing an impartial and effective selection procedure that enhances wireless sensor network energy efficiency overall.

2.2.2 Trust-Based Routing

• TAODV

Authors in [98]) outlined a model that is a novel trust-based protocol by extending AODV (ad-hoc on-demand distance vector), which protocol is highly in use by many other researchers. TAODV (trusted ad-hoc on-demand distance vector) is proposed by the author and is used by the mobile nodes in an ad-hoc network. This can work dynamically and has a lot many advantages such as processing time being comparatively less, memory overhead being reduced, and less network utilization. TAODV never maintains routes for inactive nodes but it permits the distant nodes to quickly acquire routes for new destinations. It is a routing protocol that deals with table management. Even the information of short-lived nodes must be kept safely in the route table. It is mandatory to manage sequence numbers to avoid the nodes slipping into looping. Information about the sequence number is stored safely in the route table even after the node is unreachable or deactivated. Certainly, the destination of dead nodes becomes dismantled. Once this type of situation arises, the route is invalidated so that it will not be used in some other operations and the sequence number associated with this is marked as invalid. TAODV applies a trust model to advocate the routing nodes that are trusted and it also enhances the security.

• VAR over Backpressure Protocol

A trust model namely Vector Auto Regression (VAR) over Backpressure Protocol was applied in [170]. In the Backpressure algorithm, it is assumed that every node in the network cooperates to carry forward the traffic of the network that's why this algorithm is throughput optimal. However, this concept is not possible in reality, especially in the presence of malicious nodes. So, the autoregression technique is developed to implant trust between the link weights which makes it more likely for trusted links to be programmed. With the help VAR trust model, nodes in WSN can learn quickly about the behavior of malicious nodes and it immediately changes the path of the packet for successful routing. It leads to an increase in the overall performance of the system.

• Beta-based Trust and Reputation System

A Beta-based trust and reputation system for WSN was introduced in [5]. If a node needs to communicate with some other node in the network then it computes its reputation trust value based on historical events of that node. The value obtained through this method is direct trust value and indirect trust value can only be calculated by sending a signal to all the nodes present in the network. Communication trust and data trust are considered in this system. By setting the weights and threshold values, this technique protects the system from defamed and collision attacks.

- **Quality of Service**

Authors of paper [119] presented a QoS (Quality of Service) routing algorithm to calculate the credibility of the routing nodes. This algorithm directly counts the quality of service trust of 1-hop for neighbor routing nodes and the 2-hop neighbour routing node's indirect trust is calculated by the transitive rule (eg. X believes in Y and Y believes in Z then X believes in Z). Some parameters like bandwidth, mobility, and node residual energy are being considered while evaluating the QoS trust. In this model, trust is developed in four steps i.e. Computation, aggregation, propagation, and routing. QoS information of every node present in the network is stored by each node in the form of trust matrices. Matrix operations from source to destination are being performed in search of trustworthy nodes.

- **Active Trust Model**

Authors in [102] came forth with an active detection-based security and trust routing scheme named Active Trust model for Wireless Sensor Networks. Active trust is capable of blocking various attacks especially blackhole and grayhole attacks in WSN. It creates various paths to detect the nodal trust to improve security. In a blackhole attack, a malicious node never passes the data rather it consumes the packet while in a grayhole attack, it selects the normal data and forwards it to the next node.

- **Virtual Trust Queuing Model**

In paper [103], authors proposed a virtual trust queuing model in order to repeal the limitations of the backpressure algorithm. In this, the behaviour of routing nodes is quantified and recorded according to the algorithm-compliance. This scheme can work in a dynamic environment and supports multi-hop networks to provide better throughput in routing. The author constructs a virtual trust queue that can support the deviations of a node from expected algorithm outcomes. Along with the back-pressure algorithm, if the virtual trust queue and real packet queue work then it will not only retain flexibility rather it increase throughput under security threats.

• **Bayesian based Trust Management Scheme**

A Bayesian-based trust management scheme (BTMS) was proposed by authors in [18], that enables a user to compute the direct and indirect trust value of each vertex in WSN. Bayesian equation is used to devise the direct trust values while indirect trust values are computed by using the mechanism of calling these values when there is no direct trust value. A new factor called the self-confidence factor is introduced to calculate the aggregated trust values that assign different weights to the recommenders according to their reputation. This reduces the trust value of malicious nodes in the network because node selection by the recommender is done with high efficiency.

• **Maximum Benefit Function**

Authors in paper [138] submitted an efficient routing protocol in a Wireless body area network to perform reliable data transmission. They consider many parameters like residual energy, transmission efficiency, available bandwidth, and number of hops to the sink node. A maximum benefit function to select 'the next hop node by normalizing the node parameters and selecting the node with the largest value as the next hop node. The proposed work is compared with a priority-based energy-efficient routing algorithm (PERA) which shows an improvement in the reliability of data transmission.

• **FBCR**

Authors of paper [118] included network zoning and several node factors such as residual energy, distance to the center of each zone, and the node-to-base station angle, a unique clustering routing protocol utilizing fuzzy logic was presented. This protocol uses a fuzzy-based decision-making strategy to improve the selection of cluster heads. This novel approach assigns the Base Station (BS) the duty of selecting cluster heads in each zone, defining the area for each node, calculating the distance between each node and the zone center, and calculating the angle of each node. The main goal is to systematically lower the energy consumption of the network, with a focus on role allocation that is both intelligent and strategic to maximize the routing protocol's overall efficiency.

2.2.3 Blockchain-Based Routing

• Secure Blockchain Trust Management

Authors in [52] proposed a trust management system i.e. Secure Blockchain Trust Management (SBTM), that incorporates a blockchain-based Public Key Infrastructure (PKI) for safe operations in WSN. This blockchain-based trust management system can dispense numerous advantages over conventional systems for inter-domain routing protocols. The pivotal task accomplished with SBTM is to facilitate the gradual deployment across autonomous systems with minimum cost either operational or economical. SBTM facilitates the system with better security solutions, identities of management for routing entities, digital signatures, and passwords. Public Key Infrastructure (PKI) or web of trust-based approaches with a blockchain protocol was replaced to achieve this. The use of blockchain technology completely makes the system decentralized which removes the existing centralized authorities which were more vulnerable.

• Multi-link Concurrent Communication Model

In [95], authors first established a multi-link concurrent communication model based on trust degree and then submitted a novel integrated factor communication tree algorithm (IFT). In the algorithm, nodes are categorized into three types: honest nodes, free-rider nodes, and malicious nodes according to the behavioral characteristics of nodes in blockchain-based communication. It also considered the overall node communication link number and the node trust degree. Then various trustworthy nodes with good communication capabilities are chosen to enhance the concurrency and efficiency. The proposed algorithm can reasonably deploy a routing scheme for blockchain-based communication.

• Static and Oppressive Smart Contracts

A secure framework for the Internet of Things (IoT) network by using the static and oppressive smart contracts of blockchain with a conventional cloud framework was proposed by authors in [9]. In this, metadata of cryptographic hash about gadgets is placed in the blockchain while definite data is not kept on the blockchain, rather it is stored in the cloud which makes it more flexible for the deployment of devices in WSN. Legions of smart contracts are placed in blockchain that ensure data storage in the cloud.

• **FabRec**

Authors in paper [13] came up with a decentralized approach called 'FabRec' that can control the information generated by various manufacturers with the use of blockchain technology. Due to the decentralized network, manufacturing machines and nodes for the computation of an organization become transparent and verification of third parties can be done through their past performance. Moreover, it derives an automated mechanism of smart contracts between two parties. FabRec model uses the proof of concept consensus mechanism to link the nodes for computation and other gadgets to check the feasibility of nodes present in the network.

• **Blockchain-based Contractual Routing**

Authors of [142] developed a novel blockchain-based contractual routing (BCR) protocol for a network of entrusted IoT devices. As this protocol is based on blockchain technology, no central authority is required to provide the identification and authentication of each device, this contractual routing protocol works in a decentralized environment. It uses smart contracts to find a new path from source to destination within different WSNs. The performance of the BCR protocol is compared to the AODV. The results show that the BCR reduces the routing overhead as compared to the AODV. BCR is unaffected by Greyhole and Blackhole attacks. The blockchain-based contractual routing protocol can also be utilized in ad-hoc IoT networks.

• **ATEAR**

The human psychological and physical data (Blood pressure, ECG, temperature, sugar level, etc.) from the patients that demand secure, optimal, and efficient routing techniques were collected by authors in [153]. A blockchain-based Adaptive Thermal/ Energy-Aware Routing (ATEAR) protocol is used for data transmission.

Temperature rise, throughput, and energy consumption are used to evaluate the performance of ATEAR whereas resource utilization, latency, and transaction throughput are used to investigate BC performance.

• **Private Cloud Data Centre**
Authors of paper [63] proposed a technique to improve the security of data in blockchain-based WSNs. They use microcontrollers to interconnect various sensor nodes and security is being enhanced by utilizing blockchain technology. In this, the proposed system acts as a private cloud data center that visualizes the data uploaded by the sensors to create charts and tables. The integration of blockchain technology with wireless sensor networks is thoroughly explained in this paper. To simplify blockchain security, they shift the encryption method from asymmetric to symmetric.

• **Novel Efficient Approach for Authentication**
A novel efficient approach for authentication using blockchain technology to secure the routing data in Wireless Sensor Networks was presented in [116]. Base stations, sink nodes, and normal nodes are being formulated for simulation purposes. A hybrid model is made by integrating the blockchain technology with WSN in which user authentication and verification are done through BC.

• **Blockchain-based Authentication**
Authors of [124] presented the framework for deploying Blockchain in WSN. Attackers can attack the network to get the desired information from the network. The main purpose of this paper is to reduce the attacks from hackers and improve efficiency by detecting malicious nodes. Blockchain has decentralized consensus mechanisms that help in preventing data tampering. The most modern security and data storage technology available nowadays is blockchain. Moreover, BC is managed by all the nodes of the network, and an authentication message is broadcast to each node in the network.

• **Novel Hierarchical Framework**
In [28], authors presented a novel hierarchical framework for resource slicing in 5G radio access network (RAN) to trade resources among blockchain-based mobile virtual network operators (MVNOs). A consortium blockchain network supporting

hyper-ledger smart contracts was utilized to make the trading secure among seller and buyer MVNOs. To design a fair incentive mechanism, the pricing and demand problem of seller and buyer was prototyped as a game where seller MVNO was a leader and buyer MVNO was a follower. A dueling deep Q network is developed to achieve optimal results.

• **Blockchain hor Healthcare** Authors in [51] secured information accountability and integrity in healthcare using BC. Sensor devices are prone to attacks as they are low-capability devices. Blockchain provides WSN security features along with data breach prevention methods. The majority of the nodes in WSN are low-powered devices so they may or may not be suitable for deployment in BC. In healthcare, extremely sensitive data is passed through the sensors, and altering data by malicious nodes can be lethal to the patient's life. Future cloud computing and fog computing will use BC to protect WSN transmission.

• **Blockchain-based Encryption and Trust Evaluation Model**
A blockchain-based encryption and trust evaluation model was proposed in [16], in which aggregator nodes and sensor nodes are stored. Authentication of AN (Aggregator nodes) is checked by the public blockchain whereas SN's (Sensor nodes) authentication is performed by the private blockchain. SNs are more prone to attacks because they are of low power, have less transmission range, and limited computational capabilities. PDR is high when there is a large number of trusted SNs but PDR is low when most of the SNs die due to low energy and only a few SNs participate. Rivest-Shamir-Adleman (RSA) is used for encryption and decryption of data for secure transmission.

• **Blockchain-based Authentication and Cluster Head Selection**
Authors of paper [132] proposed the security mechanism in blockchain-based WSNs by using authentication and cluster head selection. Cluster heads receive the data from the sensor nodes and process it according to the requirement. DDR-LEACHE can be substituted with CHs if the distance of BS, residual energy, and degree are considered. Many computational resources and power were needed to implement PoW so it was replaced by PoA. In the end, MITM and Sybil were used to calculate the results and check the system's resilience.

2.2.4 Blockchain-based Routing Using Reinforcement Learning

• **Blockchain Based Routing using RL**

In [178], authors proposed a blockchain-based routing scheme using reinforcement learning to ensure security and improve the performance of the network. Blockchain tokens are utilized to represent packets and validator nodes confirm transactions to release them in the network. A dynamic and trusted routing information can be obtained by the nodes on the blockchain-based decentralized network where every transaction is traceable and tamper-proof. Then reinforcement learning algorithm is applied for better path selection and to avoid malicious nodes. Results show better latency and throughput and also suppress the attacks of malicious nodes on the network.

• **Novel Trust Model**

A novel trust model for routing based on Blockchain with reinforcement learning was introduced in [159]. Blockchain is a decentralized system so it provides an optimal mechanism for routing information management and also provides a platform to schedule routing for reinforcement learning. In this tokens are used to represent the routing packets and the transaction of every routing is released to the network with the acknowledgement of validated nodes. After making each transaction secure and reachable, routing nodes can get time-to-time routing information on the blockchain network.

• **Universal Model Free Deep RL**

Authors in [174] proposed a universal model-free deep RL for computing resource providers and customers. They resolve auction problems by implementing pricing and resource allocation. Three questions are answered in this paper: 1. How does the auction mechanism run fairly? 2. How to fairly assign resources of providers to customers? 3. How to make each participator engage in bidding strategies? A blockchain-based computer resource trading system for pricing and bidding is developed to make trading secure, safe, and effective. The proposed DRL performed much better than other systems.

• Q-Learning to Minimize Forking

The usage of the Reinforcement learning techniques to address the challenges that Blockchain-based networks face was highlighted in [69]. Mainly this paper has emphasized on minimizing the forking events using the Q-learning technique. Moreover, open challenges in blockchain-enabled networks and future work are discussed in detail. First of all, energy constraint is the major issue in applying RL to blockchain because low-powered devices drain energy very quickly. Secondly, RL and blockchain work independently which is why it creates communication problems and hence degrades the performance of the network. Thirdly, scalability issues in blockchain become more complex with RL. Lastly, financial forecasting and the selection of appropriate RL techniques are other issues in this type of network.

• Novel Cooperative Task Offloading and Blockchain Mining

Authors of paper [123] proposed a novel cooperative task offloading and blockchain mining (TOBM) for blockchain-based mobile edge computing (MEC) systems to enhance security. To tackle with latency problem in MEC because of blockchain operation, they developed a new consensus mechanism called proof of reputation (PoW). Moreover, to deal with the dynamic environment and high dimensional system state space, they develop novel distributed deep reinforcement learning.

• DRLBTS

A deep reinforcement learning aware blockchain-based task scheduling (DRLBTS) to provide security and efficient scheduling to healthcare applications was proposed in [91]. The existing system deals with security, task scheduling, and processing costs of healthcare paradigms. DRBLTS solves the scheduling problem on different computing nodes for the workflows. The first deep Q-learning approach divides the problem into different categories. Then these tasks are further distributed to fog, mobile, and cloud-based systems. All the failure tasks are handled with adaptive Q-learning and rescheduled on available computing nodes.

• Blockchain-based Trust Mechanism

Authors prevented selfish edge attacks and faked service road attacks in Mobile Edge Computing by using a blockchain-based trust mechanism [97]. The computational performance of edge devices is broadcasted to the whole network by using a trust mechanism. PoW (Proof of Work) and PoS (Proof of Stake) are the consensus protocols that are being utilized to append a block onto the MEC blockchain. A deep reinforcement learning algorithm is proposed to improve the performance. The final results show that the proposed model successfully handles the attacks and improves the latency and energy efficiency of the system.

• **BLOR**

Authors in [67] proposed BLOR (Bayesian Learning Oracles Reliability) mechanism to recognize trust-less and cost-efficient oracles. Smart contracts can't operate directly on data that is residing on the blockchain so they need oracles to help smart contracts with the blockchain system. All the oracles are not trustworthy, some of them can be malicious. By using BLOR, they learn oracle behaviour and RL guides them in the learning process. Outcomes clearly show that BLOR is much better at selecting reliable and economical oracles.

• **Blockchain with RL**

The blockchain technology was integrated with reinforcement learning to detect attacks in IoT networks and to enhance network security and resilience [149]. The decentralized and transparent nature of blockchain combined with RL has better decision-making capabilities to make the network robust and attack-free. The main components of the design were described by the authors such as blockchain infrastructure, device interaction, attack detection model, network consensus, blockchain-RL integration, etc. Simulation results show the efficiency of the network by detecting attacks and reducing risks.

• **RLBEEP**

Authors in [1] proposed RLBEEP (Reinforcement-Learning-Based Energy Efficient Control and Routing Protocol for Wireless Sensor Networks). The authors proposed three energy management approaches to improve the lifetime of wireless sensor networks. Firstly, reinforcement learning is utilized to minimize route length and reduce energy consumption. Secondly, a sleep scheduling technique is utilized to improve node energy consumption. Lastly, data transmission of each node is restricted based on the received data change rate.

• ReLeC

The Reinforcement Learning-based and Clustering-enhanced (ReLeC) method for energy optimization in Wireless Sensor Networks (WSN) was introduced in [59]. The ReLeC protocol aims to improve energy efficiency by enabling sensor nodes to make informed decisions through the exchange of local information with neighboring nodes. It focuses on enhancing next-hop selection to reduce energy consumption. The protocol achieves this by modifying the routing tables of neighboring nodes based on the packet header contents of sensor nodes, with the sender including local data such as node IDs, remaining energy, and node coordinates in the packet header. The ReLeC protocol operates similarly to other clustering-based protocols and consists of three key phases:

a. Network Initialization

b. Cluster Head (CH) election and Cluster creation

c. The Communication phase

Table 2.1 shows various routing techniques and protocols that provide unique advantages suited to the particular requirements of computer networks. These benefits include adaptation to changing network conditions, fault tolerance, scalability, efficiency, and energy economy. Effective protocols decrease delay, maximize resource utilization, and minimize overhead. Scalable protocols, which frequently use distributed or hierarchical techniques, allow networks to expand without experiencing performance loss. Resilience is ensured by fault-tolerant protocols, which quickly identify and reroute traffic around malfunctions. Energy-efficient protocols prolong the life of device batteries by saving power, especially in wireless situations. Protocols that exhibit adaptability to dynamic settings can optimize performance in a variety of scenarios by modifying routing decisions in response to real-time input.

Table 2.1: Existing Routing Approaches

Reference	**Year**	**Routing Protocol**	**Benefits**
Al-Rawi *et al.* [5]	2013	Beta-based trust and reputation system	Defends collision attacks
Lu *et al.*[103]	2015	Virtual trust queuing model	Throughput, Relaibility
Liu *et al.* [102]	2016	Active Trust model	Defends black hole attack, Network Lifetime
Nageswarao *et al.* [119]	2016	QoS (Quality of Service) routing algorithm	Improve Performance, Resource Optimization
Li *et al.* [98]	2017	TAODV (trusted ad-hoc on-demand distance vector)	Reduces Computational Overhead
Gomez-Arevalillo *et al.* [52]	2017	Secure Blockchain Trust Management (SBTM)	Enhanced Security, Reduce Computational Cost
Bach *et al.* [18]	2018	Bayesian based trust management scheme (BTMS)	Reliability, Security
Ramezan *et al.* [142]	2018	Blockchain-based contractual routing (BCR)	Latency, Throughput, PDR
Eshrkawey *et al.* [46]	2022	Re-position particle swarm optimization (RPSO)	Energy Consumption, Network Lifetime
Beniata *et al.* [24]	2022	Random Neighbor Selection Protocol	Enhancement of message propagation and security
Awan *et al.* [16]	2022	Blockchain authentication and trust module	High Packet Delivery Ratio

2.3 Problem Definition

Based on the above literature review, it is observed that even though a lot of research, for routing data in Wireless Sensor Networks, has already been done to enhance security and optimize energy efficiency yet a plenty of gaps have been discovered in these traditional methods. Most of the systems were centralized in which all the nodes in the network needed to have relied on the central authority for transmitting data from one node to another. So, a decentralized network is needed through which nodes can communicate directly with each other. Blockchain technology fits better to overcome the above issue because it is a decentralized, distributed, and tamper-proof system. Moreover, low-powered sensor nodes in WSN have limited storage capacity hence it degrades the overall performance of the network. Blockchain, with unlimited storage and better alternatives to enhance security, is the better option to replace conventional centralized networks. Different consensus mechanisms are available as per the requirement of the network and user to guard the network against different types of attacks.

However, various business areas and research fields associated with blockchain technology provide a lot of opportunities to work but it still faces many problems in routing schemes and maintaining the security of the network. It is not an easy task to select a consensus mechanism because there are numerous mechanisms available nowadays, for example- PoW, PoS, PoA, etc. Blockchain doesn't need any authorization and everybody can join the network, so one needs to interact with unknowns that's why security is the foremost concern in this system.

Apart from this, various learning models are accessible nowadays, such as machine learning (ML), deep learning (DL), reinforcement learning, etc. Reinforcement learning is utilized to select the optimal paths by dynamically learning from the environment. Efforts have been made to attain the desired outcomes by developing an updated reinforcement learning model in conjunction with the LEACH protocol at every routing node. This collaborative approach aims to enhance the trustworthiness of the network for its users.

Although, a variety of software and tools are available to develop a blockchain-based WSN using RL but MATLAB and Python were found to be perfect to fulfil the requirements of the proposed task.

2.4 Research Objectives

- To study and analyze the state of the art of blockchain-based models with Reinforcement Learning for Wireless Sensor Networks to identify security issues.
- To propose and implement a secure blockchain-based wireless sensor network model.
- To propose and implement a reinforcement learning method to improve the energy efficiency of the proposed blockchain-based secure wireless sensor network model.
- To evaluate and compare the proposed model using standard metrics.

2.5 Conclusion

An extensive literature review on traditional as well as current blockchain-based models in Wireless Sensor Networks has been presented in this chapter. A lot of work has already been done to ensure energy efficiency and security in Wireless Sensor Networks. A decentralized technology, blockchain, was found to be an effective solution in terms of security to substitute it with traditional centralized models and various blockchain-based models are discussed in the chapter. Moreover, a variety of learning approaches are available nowadays to make routing decisions more efficient and the newest approach Reinforcement learning seems to be the best technique in which the system learns from itself dynamically. So, numerous blockchain-based models using reinforcement learning for WSN have been revealed and discussed in this chapter. In the end, this chapter also addresses the problem definition and outlines the research objectives.

Chapter 3

Issues in Existing WSN Models

3.1 Challenges in WSN

Wireless Sensor Networks (WSNs) are essential for many applications, including surveillance, medical, agriculture, and environmental monitoring. To increase the effectiveness, dependability, and security of these networks, researchers are working to resolve several problems that current WSN models must contend with.

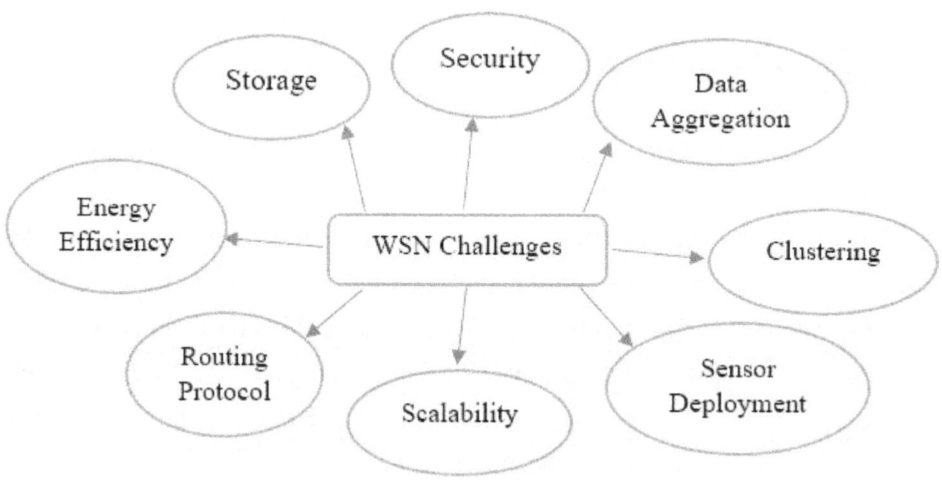

Figure 3.1: WSN Challenges

Based on the literature survey, Figure 3.1 shows various challenges in WSN.

• Scalability

The number of sensor devices is increasing rapidly in Wireless Sensor Networks. These devices are generally utilized for tracking, monitoring, and controlling. Networks collect the data from the nodes and serve this information to the specific user. The protocol employed for data routing must demonstrate adaptability to potential changes within the Wireless Sensor Network. The network is said to be scalable if it adapts to the changes that occur due to more nodes at a later stage after design. [86] observed that the BVR protocol is the efficient protocol for scalability

• Energy Efficiency

Energy is one of the most critical resources in the WSNs to be controlled to enhance the lifetime of the network. Sensor devices have limited power and they need to send sensitive data from one node to another. Collision, overhearing, packet overhead, etc. are the main reasons to deplete the maximum energy of the network. [127] presents many energy-saving techniques like duty cycling, data reduction schemes, mobile sinks, mobile relays, etc.

• Storage

In WSNs, nodes fail because of the low hardware quality, limited storage, natural disasters, less power, and attacks. Nodes in WSN need to transmit data regularly but sometimes they are capable of handling the load of data because of less storage capacity. There are three data storage and retrieval methods [3] referred to as External Storage (ES), Local Storage (LS), and Data-Centric Storage (DCS).

• Data Aggregation

Data aggregation is a widely used technique in wireless sensor networks. In WSNs, data is coming from many sensor nodes and this needs to be aggregated as if they are about the same attribute of the phenomenon when they reach the same routing node on the way back to the sink. Most of the aggregation schemes involve reducing the amount of power consumed throughout data transmission between the sensor nodes. Two security pillars, confidentiality, and integrity, are compromised during data aggregation [40].

• Security

One of the major challenges in WSN is to provide high security with restricted resources. Security requirements in Wireless Sensor Networks consist of node authentication, confidentiality of data, and resilience against traffic. There can be both, trustworthy and malicious, nodes present in the network and to identify these, node authentication examination is needed through which unreliable nodes will be kicked out of the network [94].

• Sensor Deployment

Optimizing coverage and connectivity is a major prerequisite for the efficient performance of WSNs. Coverage gives a measure of how well sensor nodes are detecting any event in the region where they are dispersed. Two deployment methods in wireless sensor networks are deterministic-based deployment and random deployment. In deterministic-based deployment model covers the full area of the environment even if man-made deployment is difficult. In the random deployment method, the full coverage of a particular environment is difficult but this model is economical [133].

• Routing Protocol

To design routing protocols for WSN is a difficult task because of multiple characteristics, which differentiate them, from wireless infrastructure-less networks. There are some issues while routing in WSN. Firstly, it is quite challenging to allocate a universal identifier scheme for a large number of sensor nodes. Secondly, the whole data collected by sensor nodes is to be sent to a particular base station. Thirdly, sensors can sense the same data repeatedly so there can be the chances of redundancy. Lastly, Sensor nodes can have different energy, bandwidth, capacity, etc. so routing protocols need to be designed to cope with these dissimilarities [152].

• Clustering

Clustering is the common topology technique in Wireless Sensor Networks. Apart from energy efficiency, clustering can resolve plenty of networking matters like load balancing, QoS, security, and mobility management. Nowadays, most of the networks are heterogeneous so it is not an easy task that every clustering mechanism will support these networks. [154] presents various clustering techniques like LEACH, HEED, etc.

3.2 Security issues in Existing Blockchain-based Technologies for WSN

Wireless Sensor Networks (WSNs) with a blockchain foundation offer a secure, decentralized framework for data exchange and management. However, it also confronts several difficulties and problems, which researchers are attempting to resolve.

Table 3.1 provides a comprehensive overview of various mechanisms and their associated issues in the context of network security. In the surveillance Wireless Sensor Networks (SWSNs) proposed by Sert *et al.* [151], the primary concern is an increased vulnerability to security attacks, potentially jeopardizing the network's integrity. Wang *et al.* [172] provided data sharing scheme, utilizing Blockchain technology, is criticized for having a low-verification process, which could compromise overall system security. Similarly, Ghaleb *et al.* [49] proposed SecRPL routing protocol for a deficient verification process, raising concerns about the reliability of data transmission. "EdgeChain," a system based on blockchain and smart contracts proposed by Pan *et al.* [128], is deemed insecure for handling private data, posing a threat to data privacy. Yang *et al.* [179] presented that blockchain privacy-preservation crowdsensing system faces the risk of attacks by unidentified individuals during data transmission. Nicolas *et al.* [126] introduced Multistage Secure Pool encounters complications in data transactions, indicating potential challenges in maintaining a secure data flow. Bhushan *et al.* [27] proposed a transaction privacy preservation mechanism for blockchain technology, but it lacks assurance in safeguarding data privacy. Qiu *et al.* [137] suggested a novel location privacy-preserving approach based on blockchain that is criticized for weaknesses in protecting private information. Finally, Al-Shammari *et al.* [6] presented a framework for secure healthcare applications that face security concerns, including the risk of dropping any node data during transmission, compromising the integrity of healthcare information.

Table 3.1: Security issues in existing Blockchain-based technologies for WSN

Reference	**Year**	**Mechanism**	**Issue**
Sert *et al.* [151]	2015	Surveillance Wireless Sensor Networks (SWSNs)	More chances of security attacks
Wang *et al.* [172]	2018	Data Sharing Scheme based on Blockchain technology	The verification process is low
Ghaleb *et al.* [49]	2018	SecRPL (Routing Protocol for Low-power and Lossy Networks)	The verification process is low
Pan *et al.* [128]	2018	"EdgeChain" based on blockchain and smart contracts	Not secure for private data
Yang *et al.* [179]	2019	A Blockchain privacy-preservation crowd-sensing system	An unknown person can attack transmission
Nicolas *et al.* [126]	2019	Multistage Secure Pool	The complication in data transactions
Bhushan *et al.* [27]	2020	Transaction Privacy Preservations for Blockchain Technology	No assurance of privacy of data
Qiu *et al.* [137]	2020	A Novel Location Privacy-Preserving Approach Based on Blockchain	Weakness of private information
Al-Shammari *et al.* [6]	2021	A framework and prototype for secure healthcare application processing via blockchain using deep learning	Not secure, any node data can be dropped during transmission.

3.3 Security Issues in Blockchain-based Models Using Reinforcement Learning

There are more complications and difficulties when blockchain technology is integrated with Wireless Sensor Networks (WSNs) and reinforcement learning. Although this combination may be advantageous, there are a number of problems with current blockchain-based WSN models that use reinforcement learning. Some of these issues are discussed below:

To assess the content of messages received from other cars directly, [55] presented a novel trust model. The model is constructed using several different parameters, including route similarity, content conflict, and similarity of content. The message content's credibility will be assessed at the vehicle level and won't impose any new architectural presumptions. This paper successfully fixed the authentication problem, however, it didn't check the integrity of the message.

[144] provided a deep learning (DL) and blockchain-powered security framework for intelligent 5G-enabled Internet of Things (IoT) that makes use of blockchain for data security and DL competency for intelligent data analysis operations. The hierarchical design of the framework was shown, showing how blockchain and deep learning processes arise across the four layers of cloud, fog, edge, and user. To confirm the suggested framework's viability in real-world applications, a simulation was conducted on a popular object detection task. The simulation findings show that the proposed framework satisfies the requirements for scalability, reliability and performance, QoS, computational complexity, security and privacy, and QoE—all essential elements of design and development in an IoT environment provided by 5G. However, it resolved the problem of breach and loss of sensitive data but computational complexity problems still exist there.

[141] provided a layered hierarchical architecture that can be used to create a Blockchain-enabled SDN-IoT framework that is distributed but effective. This framework guaranteed safe network communication and effective cluster-head selection by identifying and isolating rouge switches. Additionally, the consistency within the controller cluster was maintained and the rules implemented in the switches are tracked by the Blockchain-enabled flow-rules record. Lastly, they evaluated the suggested framework's performance in a simulation environment and demonstrated its ability to optimize energy utilization, end-to-end delay, and throughput in comparison to baselines taken into consideration, hence achieving security and efficiency in the smart network. The major drawback of this method was that large-scale integration was not considered while designing.

[65] provided a distributed and decentralized blockchain Software-defined networking (SDN) based energy-aware architecture for the Internet of Things (IoT) in smart cities in order to address various problems. SDN continuously monitors, regulates, and oversees the actions of IoT devices and looks for potential network assaults; Blockchain eliminates central point of failure problems and offers sufficient protection and privacy against cyberattacks; Network Function Virtualization (NFV) was utilized for energy conservation and load balancing, as well as extending the life of the network. To lower the energy usage in the model that was being provided, they also proposed the Cluster Head Selection (CHS) algorithm. Time complexity of this algorithm was very high.

[72] described an SDN-enabled architecture that takes into account the resource-constrained IoT devices so as not to burden them and uses hybrid deep learning detection algorithms for the effective detection of cyber threats and attacks. They train algorithms using the cutting-edge CICDDoS 2019 dataset. This algorithm produces findings that are very accurate while having a low false positive rate (FPR) and testing time. IoT devices with limited resources were employed in this, however they were unable to offer any low-cost computing or storage mechanisms.

[84] suggested a blockchain-based trust management approach to improve the trust relationships between beacon nodes and eliminate rogue nodes in Wireless Sensor Networks (WSNs). Both data-based and behaviorally-based trust were included in

this composite trust assessment. The computation of behavioral-based trust of beacon nodes took into consideration a number of criteria, including closeness, honesty, intimacy, and frequency of interaction. In addition, each beacon node's composite trust value—which combined data and behavior—was transmitted to Base Stations (BS) in order to create a blockchain of trust values. The management approach then eliminated the beacon node with the lowest trust value, ensuring the consistency and dependability of localization in WSNs.

[43] analysed and compared five machine learning algorithms and one deep learning algorithm to detect and prevent various attacks like greyhole, blackhole, TDMA scheduling and flooding which come under the category of DoS attacks. Moreover, they utilized K-fold cross-validation to get more accurate predictions. Machine Learning algorithms like Random Forest, Support Vector Machines, and Deep Learning algorithms, namely, Artificial Neural Networks are capable of detecting intrusion in the system.

Table 3.2 summarizes a number of studies that examine the relationship between blockchain technology, reinforcement learning (RL), and related mechanisms. The RLBC algorithm in Yang *et al.* combines blockchain technology and reinforcement learning; nonetheless, it faces difficulties with data validation and loses efficiency when a lot of nodes are present. The work of Jameel *et al.* presents a Q-learning method; nevertheless, since RL and blockchain function separately, there is a significant disadvantage. A universal model-free deep reinforcement learning (DRL) with blockchain is proposed by Xie *et al.*, yet there are problems with the approach's viability in dynamic contexts. Blockchain-based resource trade is the main emphasis of Boateng *et al.*, yet the approach is criticized for using a lot of resources. External security threats are encountered by Li *et al.*'s trust mechanism. The TOBM technique by Nguyen *et al.* uses a lot of energy to offload tasks. A limited defense-capable RL-based attack detection model is developed by Sangeetha *et al.* The BLOR method by Jamal *et al.* encounters randomization problems in a limited blockchain architecture. Lakhan *et al.* introduce the DRLBTS algorithm, which has overhead at several network nodes and does not enable real-time applications. Together, these works shed light on the difficulties and constraints associated with fusing blockchain technology with reinforcement learning, offering new avenues for investigation and advancement in this rapidly developing subject.

Table 3.2: Security issues in Blockchain-based models using RL for WSNs

Reference	Year	Mechanism	Issue
Yang *et al.* [178].	2019	Reinforcement Learning and Blockchain-based (RLBC) algorithm	Data not validated, Less effective with a large number of nodes
Jameel *et al.* [69]	2020	Q-Learning technique	RL and Blockchain work independently
Xie *et al.* [174]	2020	Universal model-free Deep Reinforcement Learning (DRL) with Blockchain	Less feasible in dynamic environment
Boateng *et al.* [28].	2021	Blockchain-based resource trading among P2P mobile virtual network operators (MVNOs	High Resource utilization
Li *et al.* [97]	2022	Blockchain based trust mechanism with RL	External security risks
Nguyen *et al.* [123]	2022	A novel cooperative task offloading and blockchain mining (TOBM) scheme for a blockchain-based MEC system	Much energy resources consumed for computation task offloading
Sangeetha *et al.* [149]	2023	An RL-based attack detection model	Less defence capabilities
Jamal *et al.* [67]	2023	BLOR (Bayesian Learning Oracles Reliability) mechanism	Randomness issue within the limited blockchain structure
Lakhan *et al.* [91]	2023	Deep Reinforcement learning-aware Blockchain-based Task Scheduling (DRLBTS) algorithm	Do not support real-time applications, incur overhead at different nodes

3.4 Research Gaps

During the literature survey, a few fields were discovered that have pivotal scope for further research:

- **Energy Efficiency:**
The process of electing cluster heads involves communication and computation overhead, leading to additional energy consumption. Longer communication distances may be required between nodes, which would need more energy and transmission power. Moreover, energy resources can be depleted by security attacks that force nodes to execute more computations or send extra data. To reduce overhead, optimize the cluster head selection process by using energy-aware metrics, modifying the selection threshold, or applying probabilistic techniques.

- **Computational Complexity:**
Involvement of blockchain adds better security in WSN but at the same time, computation complexity results in high energy usage. The incorporation of a learning algorithm increases the difficulty level of the whole system. Need to decrease overall complexity.

- **Selection of Consensus Mechanism:**
Still an open question about which consensus mechanism to execute in the blockchain network. A lot of consensus mechanisms are available such PoW. PoS, PoA, PoC etc. Consensus mechanisms are being chosen as per the requirement of the network Model.

- **Reliability:**
As network decisions are based on learning outcomes, the accuracy and reliability of learning models are still questionable due to dataset structure. Moreover, sensor nodes are more attack-prone in WSNs because a malicious node can knock down the whole system.

- **Network Latency:**
In a peer-to-peer network, the major issue that affects the overall performance is

latency. Before the validation, a transaction is to be broadcasted to all other nodes present in the network and consensus is made only after the response and after the agreement of at least 50 percent of nodes. If a network has only one customized bandwidth then it will decrease the amount of delays, hence improving overall system performance.

• **Power consuming gadgets in Blockchain:**
The foremost trouble to put on Reinforcement learning technique in a Blockchain-based environment is the power consumption nature of the devices. By using RL, no doubt the performance of the overall system increases but it consumes the energy of devices very quickly. When RL is used with deep learning, this problem can be enlarged. Therefore, a system is required that can optimize energy conservation within a blockchain environment when utilizing RL techniques.

• **Scalability:**
As blockchain is an open source, so umpteen number of users can join the network without any restrictions. It becomes the pivotal area of research in this peer-to-peer network. Scalability itself was the prime issue but the difficulty level increased with the introduction of RL technique because it needed instructions again and again. It becomes more troublesome when users go in and out of the network regularly.

• **Minimizing block pulse:**
The entire amount of time it takes to mine a block is called block interval. In a blockchain-enabled network, the average block time is directly proportional to the difficulty level of the consensus mechanism used in that network. That's why some currently available platforms can vary the complexity of blocks. Several methods can used to identify the complexity of the programs that depend on scale and other characteristics of the network. If the average block interval is below the anticipated block time, then it can increase the difficulty. On the other hand, if the expected block time is slighter than the average block time then the difficulty level can be reduced. Performance can be improved in a blockchain network on a variety of attributes by utilizing RL approaches.

• **Security:**

The most important aspect of blockchain networks is security because miners need to send and receive subtle information over the network. Physical layer security techniques must be stronger to tackle security issues. Q-Deep learning can be used to add artificial noise in the network to confuse the secret learners but with extra care so that it cannot affect the actual data.

• **Complexity of smart contract:**
Smart contracts, nowadays, are considered as the phenomenal part of the blockchain technology, yet so complicated especially for beginners. Smart Contract complexity is validated through two different terms: one is validation logic and another is read/write count in the ledger. Clearly, these two attributes affect the system's performance. Increment in these two leads to soaring up the latency thus it upgrades the overall throughput.

• **Transaction payload size:**
Since the transaction and its payload need to be relayed over the network to all the nodes, bigger payloads take more time for replication across nodes. So one of the best practices is to store the large payloads and documents in an off-chain storage and record their reference on blockchain.

• **Transaction pool:**
It is also called meempool where valid but unconfirmed transactions are temporarily stored. The transactions that are being verified and wait to be selected by the miners in order to get included in a block and further added to the blockchain. During high-traffic networking, this pool may grow more as transactions compete with each other to be appended on the block.

• **Number of nodes:**
As the number of nodes increases, the longer it takes for a transaction to be propagated and consensus to be achieved the more it degrades the overall performance. Techniques to reduce the communication overhead and allow nodes to rely on the validation history of a leader node and/or other peer nodes are being introduced to alleviate this problem.

The gaps in earlier work with respect to the combination of blockchain and reinforcement learning (RL) for wireless sensor networks (WSN), based on recent studies:

• **Limited Integration for Real-time Security and Efficiency:**
Most existing routing schemes focus on improving trustworthiness and security using cryptographic systems or centralized routing decisions. However, they fall short in dynamically identifying untrusted behaviors and preventing malicious node attacks effectively [177].

• **Underutilization of Reinforcement Learning Techniques:** While reinforcement learning has shown promise in enhancing network performance, its full potential in optimizing blockchain-enabled WSNs, particularly in dynamic and hostile environments, has not been fully explored [68].

• **Inadequate Focus on Distributed Node Management:**
Many solutions do not adequately leverage distributed management techniques, which are crucial for handling the dynamic nature and distributed control requirements of WSNs effectively [57].

• **Lack of Comprehensive Evaluation Metrics:**
Existing studies often lack comprehensive performance metrics to evaluate the effectiveness of combined blockchain and RL solutions in terms of latency, energy consumption, and throughput, which are crucial for practical deployments [145].

• **Challenges in Consensus Mechanism Optimization:**
Existing blockchain consensus mechanisms used in WSNs often result in high latency and computational overhead, necessitating the development of more efficient and lightweight consensus algorithms to improve system performance [123].

• **Isolated Approaches in Enabling Technologies:**
The current approaches to integrating mobile edge computing (MEC) with blockchain often provide isolated solutions tailored for specific services and scenarios, lacking a unified framework to address latency issues and system utility comprehensively

[123].

• Scalability and Energy Efficiency Challenges:
Many proposed blockchain-based solutions do not adequately address the scalability issues and high energy consumption inherent in WSNs. Effective techniques to optimize these parameters while maintaining security and efficiency are still needed [50].

3.5 Conclusion

To sum up, research into Wireless Sensor Networks (WSNs) has shown a variety of difficulties including those related to real-time processing, scalability, and energy consumption. A new frontier has emerged with the integration of blockchain technology into WSNs, promising improved security and decentralized data management. This combination does not, however, come without its share of difficulties. Interoperability problems, privacy issues, and security hazards also show up as major hurdles in several blockchain-based architectures intended for WSNs. Moreover, there are new difficulties that need to be carefully considered when combining blockchain-based WSN models with reinforcement learning. In these sophisticated models, energy consumption, latency, and computational complexity become crucial concerns. The problem of achieving optimal performance in balancing the learning capabilities of reinforcement algorithms with the resource limits of sensor nodes is significant. Finally, several research gaps are identified to support further studies in the field of WSNs. Although there has been progress in tackling security and energy efficiency issues, complete frameworks that incorporate blockchain, reinforcement learning, and WSNs holistically are still needed.

Chapter 4

Methodology

The proposed methodology focuses on securing and optimizing the energy efficiency of Wireless Sensor Networks (WSNs) through the integration of blockchain technology and the development of the RL-LEACH (Reinforcement Learning based LEACH) protocol. This novel approach blends Reinforcement Learning (RL) with the conventional LEACH protocol to create more efficient and secure wireless networks [161].

Phase 1: Data Collection and Initialization
In the initial phase, MATLAB is employed to gather and process routing data within WSNs. This involves setting up essential parameters like the number of nodes, the number of rounds, and energy constraints, which are critical in simulating real-world scenarios. Following data collection, blockchain technology is integrated. The data processed in MATLAB is uploaded to a blockchain platform, utilizing SHA256 encryption. This step is crucial for securing the data against threats such as Sybil attacks, thereby enhancing the overall security of the WSN.

Phase 2: Security Enhancement through Blockchain
To further bolster the security of the WSN, Proof of Work (PoW) and Proof of Authority (PoA) algorithms are implemented within the blockchain framework. These algorithms are instrumental in protecting the network against various attacks and in maintaining data integrity. The decentralized nature of blockchain enhances security, while its inherent immutability ensures the integrity of the data being managed.

Phase 3: Implementation of RL-LEACH Protocol
The third phase introduces the RL-LEACH protocol, an advanced iteration of the

traditional LEACH. This protocol incorporates RL to facilitate smarter decision-making and path selection, optimizing energy usage across the network. The RL-LEACH protocol involves training a model using RL techniques, where the system learns and evolves to improve path selection. This process plays a pivotal role in enhancing routing efficiency and reducing energy consumption within the network.

Phase 4: Simulation and Evaluation In this phase, the WSN environment is simulated using MATLAB by deploying the RL-LEACH protocol within this controlled setting. The performance of the system is evaluated based on critical metrics such as node longevity, energy efficiency, and security against cyber threats. This simulation is vital for assessing the effectiveness of the proposed method in a realistic network environment.

The proposed method is divided into several parts for the integration of WSN and blockchain, the major parts of the proposed work are shown in Figure 4.1.

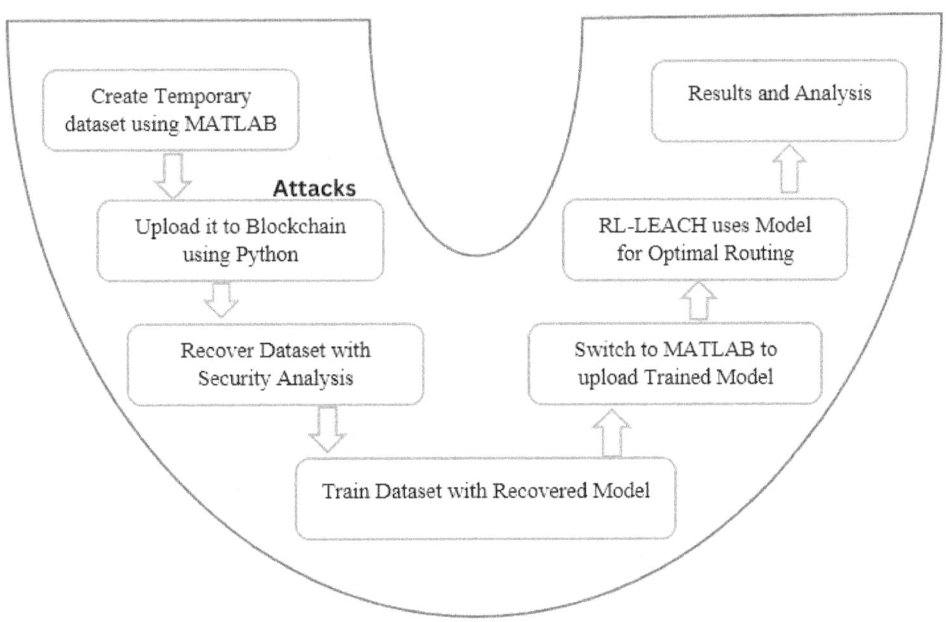

Figure 4.1: Framework of Proposed Model

4.1 Simulation Environment

To develop the proposed model, a step-by-step process was undertaken, starting with the establishment of simulation experiments in MATLAB. The data produced by MATLAB was uploaded into Python as part of the Blockchain implementation process.

Initially, a Wireless Sensor Network of 100, 200, 300, and 400 nodes with network fields of 100*100, 200*200, 300*300, and 400*400 m^2 respectively was created and various parameters being initialized such as a number of rounds, energy constants, etc. A sink node is randomly placed in the network of X and Y measured in meters. Table 4.1 depicts the environment description where four environments with different simulation areas and a number of nodes are described.

Table 4.1: Environment Description

Environment : 1	Simulation area	100*100
	Number of Nodes	100
Environment : 2	Simulation area	200*200
	Number of Nodes	200
Environment : 3	Simulation area	300*300
	Number of Nodes	300
Environment : 4	Simulation area	400*400
	Number of Nodes	400

Table 4.2: Simulation Parameters

Number of rounds	3000
Node Position	Random
Initial energy of each node	0.5 J
Sink Node coordinates	0.5*xm, 1.35*ym
Transmitter energy per node	40*0.00000001 J
Receiver energy per node	40*0.00000001 J
Data aggregation energy	4*0.00000001 J
Efs	8 * 0.000000000001 J
Emp	0.001 * 0.000000000001 J

Table 4.2 refers to various simulation parameters used in WSN:

• **Number of Rounds**
Value: 3000
This parameter acts as a number of communication rounds in the simulation. Each round typically includes data sensing, processing, and communication among sensor nodes.

• **Node Position**
Value: Random
The positions of nodes are randomly generated within the network area. This signifies that the initial deployment of sensor nodes is not determined in advance but rather distributed randomly across the specified network size.

• **Initial Energy of Each Node**
Value: 0.5 J (Joules)
Each sensor node in the network begins with an initial energy level of 0.5 Joules. This energy depicts the power available for the node to perform sensing, processing, and communication tasks throughout the simulation.

• **Sink Node Coordinates:**
Value: (0.5 * xm, 1.35 * ym)
The coordinates of the sink node need to be set at a position within the WSN area. The x-coordinate is half of the network size (0.5 * xm), and the y-coordinate is 1.35 times the network size (1.35 * ym).

• **Transmitter Energy per Node**
Value: 40 * 0.00000001 J
It is a parameter used in energy consumption calculations during communication and refers to the energy consumed by a sensor node during the transmission of data.

Receiver Energy per Node
Value: 40 * 0.00000001 J

It is used in energy consumption calculations during communication and it represents the energy consumed by a sensor node during the reception of data.

• **Data Aggregation Energy**
Value: 4 * 0.00000001 J
The process of combining and summarizing data from multiple nodes before transmitting it to the sink node is called data aggregation and the energy used in this process is data aggregation energy.

• **Efs (Free Space Energy)**
Value: 8 * 0.000000000001 J
Efs refers to the energy consumed per bit during free-space transmission and it is used in energy consumption models to estimate the energy cost of transmitting data over relatively short distances without obstacles.

• **Emp (Multi-Path Energy)**
Value: 0.001 * 0.000000000001 J
Emp refers to the energy consumed per bit during transmission in a multi-path environment and it accounts for the additional energy cost associated with signal propagation in environments with obstacles or reflections.

4.2 Data Collection and Processing

In the methodology for enhancing the security and reliability of Wireless Sensor Networks (WSNs) with blockchain technology, the process begins with data collection and processing. This initial stage involves the use of Q-tables in MATLAB to effectively gather and process the routing data. This technique allows for the structured and efficient collection of essential data for the network's operationS, ensuring that every piece of information is accounted for and organized properly.

To establish the initial parameters of the network, various elements are initialized. These include the network size, number of nodes, number of rounds, cluster heads, and energy constants. Setting these parameters is a crucial step, as based on these parameters further routing data is being stored. This approach provides a solid and reliable basis, ensuring that the network is well-defined and prepared for integration with blockchain technology.

Proper initialization and organization of these parameters contribute to the robust functioning of the WSN, supporting the overall goal of enhanced security and reliability within the network. The organized and meticulous process of data collection and initialization sets the stage for the successful application of blockchain technology to the WSN, promoting enhanced security and efficient operation throughout the network's life cycle.

Initialization Phase

Symbols Used

- N: Number of Nodes
- CH: Cluster Heads
- E_0: Initial Energy
- S: Structure Array Representing Nodes
- (xd, yd): Random Coordinates for Nodes

Algorithm: To Initialize Parameters

i. **BEGIN**
ii. Initialize Parameters N, R, CH, E_0
iii. **FOR** $i=1$ *to* N **DO**
  a. Assign Random Coordinates (xd, yd) to each node i
  b. Assign Initial energy E_0 to each node i
  c. Store node information in $S[i]$
iv. **END FOR**
v. **END**

4.2.1 WSN Configuration

The configuration of the Wireless Sensor Network (WSN) is another essential step in the proposed methodology. During this stage, each node within the network is assigned random coordinates, ensuring a diversified and extensive network layout. This distribution supports effective communication and data transmission across the entire network.

• Initialization

Along with spatial allocation, each node is assigned an initial energy level, known as E_0. This energy assignment is foundational for the network's functionality, enabling nodes to perform their tasks effectively and maintain network operations.

A sink node is identified as a central point in the network to receive data from all other nodes, ensuring efficient and centralized data accumulation. This configuration establishes a structured and organized WSN, laying the groundwork for the subsequent integration with blockchain technology and the enhancement of network security and reliability. The well-organized setup helps in the effective management and operation of the network, contributing to the overall robustness and efficiency of the WSN in the long run.

Algorithm: To Generate Data Set

i. **BEGIN**
ii. Set learning parameters α *(Learning rate)* and γ *(Discount factor)*
iii. Initialize Q table with zeros
iv. **FOR** r=1 to r_{max} **DO**
    a. Perform operations related to node clustering and energy consumption
v. **END FOR**
vi. Save Q-table as .mat file for further usage in the blockchain
vii. **END**

The network consists of sensor nodes that are deployed with a sink node located at a fixed position. The Q-learning approach is employed to make dynamic decisions regarding the routing of packets in the network. Initially, all the parameters are initialized, and then sensor nodes are deployed randomly by assigning initial energy. After that, the Q table is initialized to store Q-values for each state-action pair. Q-learning parameters (alpha and gamma) are also set to utilize them in data collection.

• **Statistics Collection**

Thereafter, the simulation is run for a specified number of rounds. At certain intervals cluster heads are being selected based on a probabilistic approach and their energy is updated accordingly. Subsequently, statistics related to dead nodes, network energy, and packets sent to sink nodes or cluster heads are collected. Q-values are updated during each round based on the current state-action pair and cost and these values are used to make further routing decisions. In the end, Q-learning data is saved to a .mat file for further analysis.

• **Data Interpretation**

Throughout the simulation rounds, the gathered statistics shed light on the energy dynamics, network performance, and Q-learning advancement. The Q-learning plot facilitates the evaluation of the learning and energy-efficient node action optimization performance of the reinforcement learning algorithm. Examining the stored Q-learning data and examining the patterns in the plotted Q-values over rounds is necessary to understand the particular outcomes. This research can shed light on how well the Q-learning algorithm converges and optimizes the behaviour of the sensor nodes in the wireless sensor network.

Figure 4.2 illustrates the progress of Q-Learning in all four environments. Tracking the sum of Q-values over several rounds of the dataset development process is the main goal. The performance and improvement of Q-Learning, are shown by the way the sum of Q-values changes over time.

The graph's x-axis shows how many rounds or iterations there are, while the y-axis shows the sum of Q-values. The graphic shows how the Q-values vary across these rounds as the dataset is created and the Q-Learning algorithm iterates through its training process.

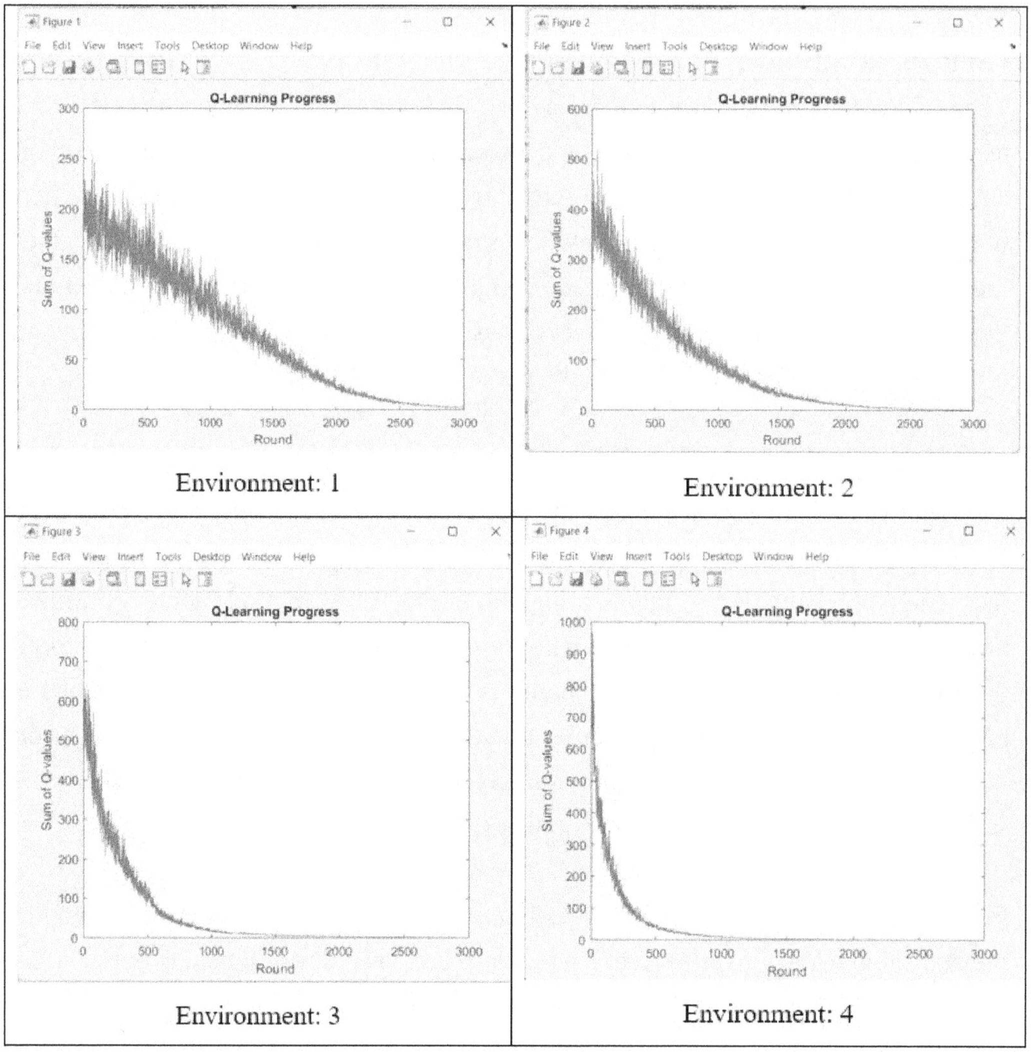

Figure 4.2: Sum of Q-values over Number of Rounds

4.3 Conclusion

The research work in this chapter presents a comprehensive approach to develop a blockchain-based model using reinforcement learning for Wireless Sensor Networks. The progression is marked by distinct phases that collectively contribute to the sophistication of the proposed model. The chapter then explores the development process and various components of a simulation environment. Furthermore, a thorough explanation of the simulation parameters provides insights into the regulated variables influencing the WSN dynamics. Subsequently, the focus shifts to the crucial phase of gathering data, which is essential to setting up the WSN by initializing its parameters. This step creates a link between theory and real-world applications allowing the model to communicate with simulated data and adjust to changing conditions. The meticulous planning of the data collection process guarantees a strong basis for the research's later stages.

Chapter 5

Integration with Blockchain

As a possible replacement for conventional centralized systems, blockchain technology has attracted a lot of interest. In the next phase, the integration with blockchain is carried out. Here's how it works: the gathered routing data, saved as a .mat file, is uploaded to the blockchain. This step is significant because the blockchain provides an extra layer of security to the stored data. The blockchain network is not centralized, meaning the data is not stored in a single location. This feature makes it hard for unauthorized persons to access or alter the data. To further enhance security, the blockchain network uses something called SHA256 cryptography encryption. This encryption method transforms the data into a code, so even if someone accesses it, they cannot understand or use the data without the correct decryption key. This two-pronged security approach—using both blockchain and SHA256 encryption—ensures that the routing data remains protected, maintaining the integrity and reliability of the entire Wireless Sensor Network.

Various tools and techniques are involved in the creation and specifying the type of blockchain. Here are the details:

• **Type of Blockchains**

The thesis employs two different types of blockchain consensus mechanisms: Proof of Authority (PoA) and Proof of Work (PoW). These consensus mechanisms determine how new blocks are added to the blockchain and how the integrity of the blockchain is maintained.

• **Creation of the Blockchain:**

• **Proof of Authority (PoA):**

• The PoA blockchain involves creating a genesis block and then adding subsequent blocks that are validated by a specific authority address. This type of blockchain is more centralized as it relies on a pre-approved authority to validate transactions.

• The blockchain is initialized with an authority address, and new blocks are created using this address to validate the blocks. The creation and validation process is managed by the Blockchain class which initializes the blockchain, creates the genesis block, and adds new blocks by calling the proof_of_authority method.

• **Key components:**

• Genesis Block Creation: create_genesis_block method.

• Block Validation: proof_of_authority method using the authority address.

• Attack Detection: Methods to detect and respond to potential attacks are included.

• **Tools:**

The implementation uses Python libraries such as hashlib for hashing, time for timestamps, and json for data encoding.

• **Proof of Work (PoW):**

The PoW blockchain involves creating a genesis block and then adding subsequent blocks that must solve a cryptographic puzzle, which is the proof of work.

• This blockchain is initialized with a difficulty level that determines the complexity of the cryptographic puzzle. Each block must find a nonce that produces a hash with a certain number of leading zeros.

• **Key components:**

• Genesis Block Creation: create_genesis_block method.

• Block Validation: proof_of_work method that involves solving the cryptographic puzzle.

• Attack Simulations: Methods to simulate various types of attacks such as Sybil, 51%, Longest Chain, Selfish Mining, and Eclipse attacks.

• **Tools:**

The implementation uses Python libraries such as hashlib for hashing, time for timestamps, and json for data encoding.

• **Process of Creation:**

• For both PoA and PoW, the process starts with creating a genesis block, which is the first block in the blockchain. Subsequent blocks are created by either validating with the authority address (PoA) or solving a cryptographic puzzle (PoW).

• The process involves reading data from a file (e.g., MATLAB .mat file), encoding the data, and then creating and adding blocks to the blockchain.

• **Tools and Techniques Used:**

• Programming Language: Python.

• Hashing: hashlib library to create SHA-256 hashes.

• Time Management: time library for timestamps.

• Data Encoding: json and base64 libraries for encoding data to be stored in the blockchain.

• Simulation and Visualization: Additional libraries such as matplotlib for plotting and reportlab for creating PDF reports (PoA only).

Two separate blockchains using different consensus mechanisms (PoW and PoA) are created in order to compare both by taking different parameters. Both consensus mechanisms efficiently handled the data upload process.

• **Data Upload Mechanism:**

The data upload mechanism in both blockchains involves reading a file (in this case, a MATLAB .mat file) and encoding its contents into a format suitable for inclusion in a blockchain block. Various steps to upload data are:

• Read the File:

The file 'Q_learning_data.mat' is read as a byte string.

• Encode the File Contents:

The byte string of the file contents is encoded into a Base64 string. This encoding ensures that the binary data can be safely included in a JSON object and subsequently stored in the blockchain.

• Prepare the Data for the Block:
The encoded file contents are included in a JSON object along with the file name. This JSON object is then converted to a string to be used as the block's data.

• Create and Add a New Block:
A new block is created with the encoded data and added to the blockchain. The block includes various fields such as index, timestamp, data, previous hash, difficulty, nonce, and hash. The block's hash is calculated using the SHA-256 algorithm, and a proof-of-work is performed to meet the specified difficulty. The mechanism ensures that the file's contents are securely and verifiably stored in the blockchain.

Figure 5.1 shows how WSN can be integrated with Blockchain, a block of blockchain is capable of storing the data of many sensors, and blocks are further connected to form a chain.

Data Set Uploading phase

Symbols Used
• *F*: .mat File
• *B*: Blockchain

Algorithm: To Upload Dataset to Blockchain

i. **BEGIN**
ii. Upload *F* to *B*
iii. Secure *B* with SHA256 cryptography encryption
iv. **END**

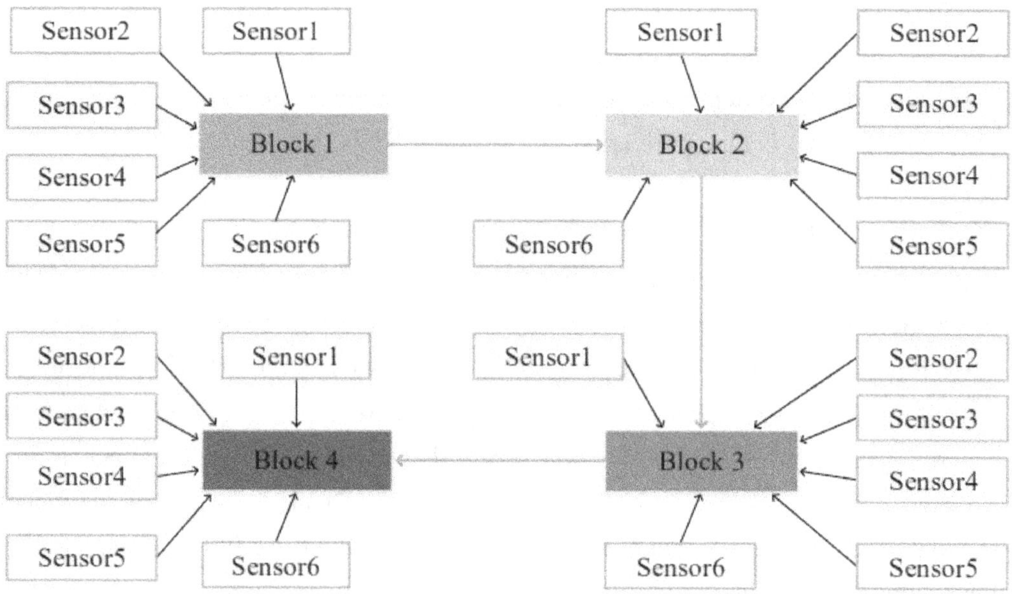

Figure 5.1: Integration of Blockchain and WSN

The proposed work implements PoA and PoW consensus mechanisms to counteract various attacks in WSNs. In the PoW mechanism, a miner is required to solve a cryptographic problem to earn the right to add a new block to the Blockchain. This process ensures that only legitimate entities can add blocks to the Blockchain, enhancing the network's security. In the PoA mechanism, a limited number of predefined nodes are granted the authority to act as validators and add new blocks to the network. This authority is vested in trusted entities, ensuring that the network remains secure from malicious attacks, including Sybil attacks [162].

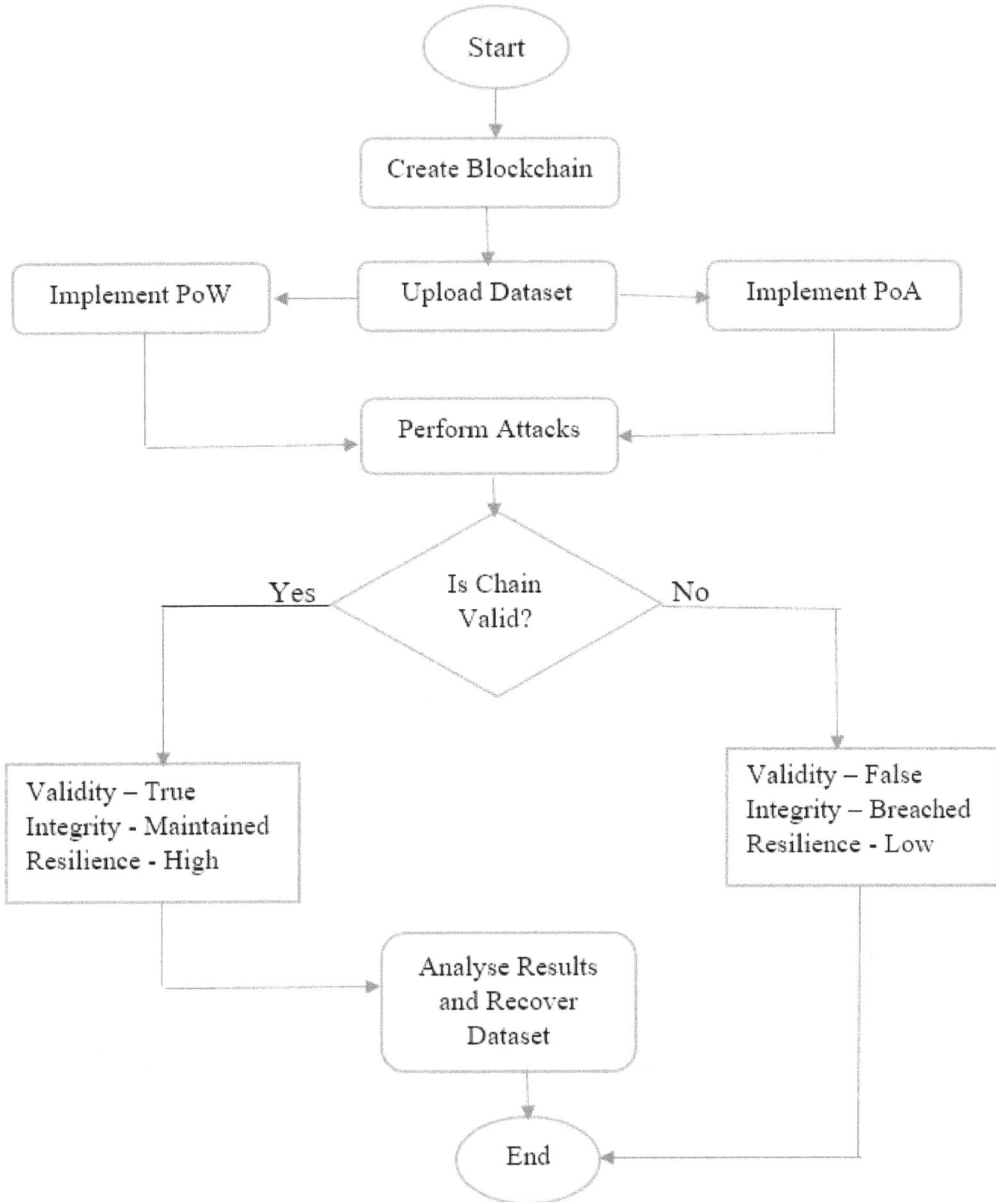

Figure 5.2: Flowchart of Blockchain Implementation

First of all, as shown in Figure 5.2, a blockchain was built in Python to carry out Proof of Work and Proof of Authority. Then, utilizing a created dataset, a series of attacks was carried out against every mechanism. After that, a procedure called is_chain_valid was run to verify the blockchain's integrity and validity.

Since the initial block (index 0) does not have a preceding block to compare it to, the function iterates all the blocks in the blockchain, starting from index 1. It retrieves both the previous block and the current block for each iteration.

Then it checks if the hash of the current block matches the hash that was determined by the "calculate_hash" method for that block. If this check is unsuccessful, the block's integrity has been compromised, which is why the procedure returns False.

To confirm the blockchain's sequence, an additional check verifies that the current block's "previous_hash" property matches the hash of the previous block to check the integrity. The procedure returns False if this check is unsuccessful.

If every block in the chain passes all checks, the method returns True, indicating that the blockchain is valid.

5.1 Implementation of PoA

Here, the basic Blockchain is implemented with a Proof of Authority consensus algorithm and simulates various types of attacks on it, including 51% attack, Sybil attack, longest chain attack, selfish mining attack, and eclipse attack.

First, a blockchain class is created that includes functions for creating blocks, adding blocks to the blockchain, checking the validity of the chain, and detecting different types of attacks.

Thereafter, a block class is created to represent individual blocks in the blockchain. Each block consists of an index, timestamp, data, a hash value, a previous hash value, and a nonce. It also includes the function to calculate the hash of the block and a function to set the nonce based on the authority address.

Then the proof_of_authority function is utilized in the block class which is a mechanism for setting the nonce attribute based on the authority address. Proof of Authority typically refers to a consensus algorithm where a participant's authority is proven by a cryptographic signature.

In the main function, the blockchain is initialized with an authority address. Then, a block is added to the blockchain that contains the data from the MATLAB .mat file encoded in base64. This data is the same which was collected as a dataset. After that, various attacks i.e. Sybil attack, 51% attack, longest chain attack, selfish mining attack, and eclipse attack are simulated, and checks the integrity of the blockchain after each attack. In the end, information about the blockchain, including block details and attack results is displayed as output.

5.2 Implementation of PoW

In this, Blockchain is implemented with a Proof of Work consensus mechanism and analyses different types of attacks. Firstly, a block class is created that represents the block of a blockchain and it contains attributes such as index, timestamp, data, previous block hash, hash of current block, and nonce.

In this, the calculate_hash function is implemented to calculate a hash and the proof_of_work function to perform proof of work and adjust the nonce to achieve a specific hash of leading zeros based on the difficulty. The calculate_hash function in the Block class is responsible for generating the hash of a block based on its attributes such as index, timestamp, data, previous hash, and nonce. It concatenates these attributes into a string and then applies the SHA-256 hashing algorithm to produce a hexadecimal hash. In proof of work, a function initializes computed_hash with the current hash using the calculate_hash function and then iteratively increments the nonce until the hash meets the difficulty criteria. Once a suitable hash is found, it updates the hash attribute of the block.

Afterward, a blockchain class is created to manage the chain of blocks. It contains the functions to add blocks to the blockchain, check the validity of the blockchain, and simulate various attacks (51% Attack, Longest Chain Attack, Selfish Mining Attack, Eclipse Attack).

Then is_chain_valid function is utilized in the Blockchain to check the integrity of the blockchain. Firstly, the genesis block is assumed to be valid and then this function iterates through the blocks in the blockchain starting from the first block to check two conditions for each pair of consecutive blocks:

Hash Consistency: It verifies that the stored hash in each block (current_block.hash) matches the hash calculated based on the block's attributes using the calculate_hash function (current_block.calculate_hash()). If there is a discrepancy, it indicates a potential tampering with the block's data.

Linking Blocks: It ensures that the previous_hash of the current block matches the hash of the previous block (previous_block.hash). This verifies that the blocks are correctly linked in the blockchain, and no block has been inserted or removed.

Then the main function initializes the blockchain with a specified difficulty. It reads the contents of the MATLAB .mat file, encodes it, and adds it as data to the blockchain. A variety of attacks are being performed including 51% attack, longest chain attack, selfish mining attack, and eclipse attack to check the validity and integrity of blockchain. In the end, data is recovered from the blockchain and again saved it as a .mat file for further use in the proposed model.

Attacks analysis

Symbols Used

· P_{PoW}: Proof of Work
· P_{PoA}: Proof of Authority
· T_{add}: Time Taken to Add Block
· T_{detect}: Attack Detection Time
· V: Blockchain Validity
· I: Blockchain Integrity
· R: Blockchain Resilience
· $T_{recovery}$: Recovery time

Algorithm: To Compare PoW and PoA

i. **BEGIN**
ii. Upload Dataset (Generated in MATLAB)

iii. Create Blockchain with P_{PoA}
iv. Perform attacks
v. Retrieve data using the Recovery Mechanism
vi. **IF** Recovered dataset size = Actual dataset generated
No Data Loss
Else
Data is compromised
vii. **END IF**
viii. Perform same for P_{PoW}
ix. Evaluate T_{add}, T_{detect}, V, I, R, $T_{recovery}$
x. Compare the results for P_{PoA} and P_{PoW}
xi. Analyze and Record Finding
xii. **END**

Figure 5.3 shows that the experiment is conducted in multiple major steps. The first step involves the creation of a blockchain by combining Proof of Work (PoW) and Proof of Authority (PoA) techniques. Once the blockchain is set up, a temporary dataset that was created at an earlier stage is uploaded and used to simulate real-world data. To evaluate the security effectiveness of both PoW and PoA, a series of attacks are applied to the blockchain. Attacks performed on the blockchain are:

- Sybil attack: An attack involving the creation of numerous fake identities to influence or manipulate the network.
- Longest Chain attack: Attempting to create a longer blockchain to override the existing legitimate chain, challenging the integrity of the system.
- 51% attack: A scenario where an entity gains control of the majority of the network's computational power, potentially compromising the integrity of the blockchain.
- Selfish Mining attack: Exploiting discrepancies in mining rewards to gain an unfair advantage in the blockchain network.
- Eclipse attack: Isolating a targeted node by controlling and manipulating its communication with the rest of the network.

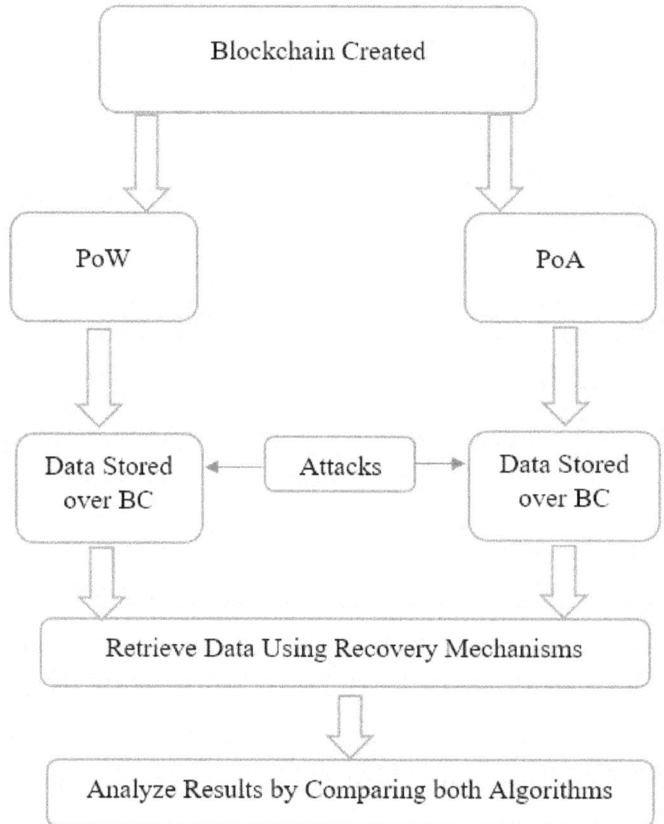

Figure 5.3: Attacks over Blockchain Network

Every attack scenario evaluates the blockchain's integrity and resilience to various threats. The system shows the efficacy of mitigation techniques by triggering recovery mechanisms to return the blockchain to a secure state after an attack. The successful recovery of the original dataset marks the experiment's conclusion and validates the resilience of the selected consensus techniques as well as the blockchain system's overall security posture.

5.3 Initial Results

Table 5.1: Comparison of key security parameters for both PoW and PoA algorithms

Security Parameter	PoW	PoA
Time taken to add block	29,423,500 nanoseconds	2,58,700 nanoseconds
Sybil Attack Detection	20,500 nanoseconds	5,500 nanoseconds
Blockchain Validity after Sybil attack	True	False
Blockchain Validity after 51% attack	True	False
Blockchain Validity after Longest Chain Attack	True	False
Blockchain Validity after Selfish Mining Attack	True	False
Blockchain Integrity after Sybil attack	Maintained	Breached
Blockchain Integrity after 51% attack	Maintained	Breached
Blockchain Integrity after Longest Chain Attack	Maintained	Breached
Blockchain Integrity after Selfish Mining Attack	Maintained	Breached
Blockchain Resilience against Sybil attack	High	Low
Blockchain Resilience against 51% attack	High	Low
Blockchain Resilience against Longest Chain Attack	High	Low
Blockchain Resilience against Selfish Mining Attack	High	Low
Eclipse attack	Target node not found	Target node not found
Recovery Time	1,600 nanoseconds	N/A

5.3.1 Detailed Analysis

Based on the results shown in Table 5.1, a detailed analysis has been conducted.

• Time to Add Block

PoW: Takes significantly longer to add a block (29,423,500 nanoseconds) due to the computational efforts required for solving cryptographic puzzles.

PoA: Much faster (258,700 nanoseconds) as it relies on pre-approved validators, reducing computational load.

• Attack Detection:

PoW: Higher detection time (20,500 nanoseconds), indicating comprehensive security checks.

PoA: Faster detection time (5,500 nanoseconds), but potentially misses intricate attack patterns due to less rigorous checks.

• Blockchain Validity and Integrity

PoW: Maintains both validity and integrity across various attacks, showcasing robustness.

PoA: Fails to uphold validity and integrity post-attacks, leading to vulnerabilities.

• Blockchain Resilience

PoW: Demonstrates high resilience, withstanding attacks and maintaining network security.

PoA: Exhibits low resilience, indicating susceptibility to security breaches.

• Recovery Time

PoW: Includes a distinct recovery mechanism with a time of 1,600 nanoseconds to restore the network post-attack.

PoA: Lacks a recovery mechanism, highlighting a significant security gap.

The comparison reveals that while PoW offers robust security features, it is less efficient in terms of time and energy consumption. PoA, on the other hand, provides faster processing and better energy efficiency but at the cost of security and resilience.

Moreover, these both algorithms can be alternatively used as per the need of user in various fields. Few examples are described below to compare PoW and PoA.

• **Healthcare Applications:**
PoW: Suitable for applications requiring high security and data integrity but may not be ideal for scenarios with limited energy resources.
PoA: Better suited for real-time applications requiring quick data validation and low latency.

• **Environmental Monitoring:**
PoW: Offers robust security but high energy consumption might limit its practicality.
PoA: Low energy consumption makes it ideal for remote environmental monitoring systems.

• **Industrial Automation:**
PoW: Provides strong security against attacks, essential for critical industrial applications.
PoA: Faster processing can enhance system performance in less critical security scenarios.

This highlights the trade-offs between PoW and PoA in blockchain applications for WSNs. PoW's strong security features make it suitable for high-security applications, while PoA's efficiency and speed are better for real-time and energy-sensitive applications. Future work could explore hybrid models that combine the strengths of both consensus mechanisms to provide balanced solutions for diverse use cases.

• **Discussion**
The comparative analysis of PoW and PoA within the realms of simulated attacks highlights crucial insights:

PoW emerges as a robust and reliable algorithm for safeguarding blockchain security. Its extensive checks, although time-consuming, contribute to enhanced security, ensuring resilience against attacks.

PoA, while efficient in terms of time, exhibits substantial vulnerabilities, particularly the absence of a solid recovery mechanism, and difficulties in maintaining blockchain validity and integrity post an attack.

The detailed evaluation and analysis underline the primacy of thoroughly assessing consensus algorithms for blockchain security within a Wireless Sensor Network. The balance between time efficiency and robust security is crucial, with PoW demonstrating enhanced security attributes, making it a preferred choice despite its time-intensive nature. On the contrary, the apparent time efficiency of PoA is overshadowed by its vulnerabilities, marking it as less suitable in scenarios demanding robust security mechanisms. This comprehensive analysis serves as a substantial guide for making informed decisions in selecting the appropriate consensus algorithm, ensuring the optimal security and efficiency of the blockchain network within the Wireless Sensor Network context.

5.3.1.1 Attacks Analysis

• **Attack Detection Mechanism**
Observation:
The system was subjected to simulated various attacks. The Proof of Work (PoW) mechanism notably took an average of 15,696 nanoseconds for attack detection and neutralization, while Proof of Authority (PoA) performed the same task in only 3,765 nanoseconds.
Analysis:
PoA's expedited detection is advantageous, yet the enduring integrity maintained by PoW, despite its extended duration, emphasizes the essentiality of a harmonized approach, merging both rapid detection and sustained post-attack integrity.

• **Blockchain Integrity Post Attack**
Observation:
After various attacks, the integrity assessment revealed PoW successfully preserving blockchain integrity, thereby preventing unauthorized alterations, unlike PoA which couldn't uphold the blockchain integrity post-attack.
Analysis:
This outcome accentuates the imperative of robust post-attack blockchain integrity,

signifying PoW's predominance in this aspect, transcending mere speedy detection.

• **Resilience Assessment**
Observation:
The assessment of resilience, quantified by the blockchain's capacity to endure and revive post-attack, depicted PoW's high resilience and unaltered functionality, in contrast to PoA's apparent operational disruption post-attack.
Analysis:
This disparity in resilience further amplifies PoW's efficacy in assuring not only attack detection but also post-attack recovery and uninterrupted operation, a quintessential factor for evaluating blockchain security

• **Data Retrieval Post-Attack**
Observation:
Post-attack data retrieval testing confirmed PoW's capability for comprehensive and accurate data recovery, while PoA unveiled data inconsistencies and loss.
Analysis:
PoW's proven ability for exhaustive data retrieval post-attack underscores its reliability and security as a steadfast blockchain operational mechanism, especially under potential adversarial assaults. These different attacks analysis within the blockchain network yields important insights regarding the network's robustness under adversarial attacks. PoW's demonstrable proficiency in timely attack detection, enduring integrity, elevated resilience, and precise data retrieval post-attack solidifies its stature as a resilient blockchain security mechanism against Sybil attacks, despite its prolonged detection timeframe. The gleaned insights not only spotlight intrinsic security attributes but also direct attention toward prospective enhancements for bolstering Sybil attack resilience and recovery in blockchain networks.

5.4 Conclusion

The integration of blockchain technology with Wireless Sensor Networks (WSN) is performed to bolster both security and reliability. It delves into the meticulous methodology of collecting routing data which is subsequently uploaded to the blockchain.

The blockchain's robust security is ensured through the utilization of SHA256 cryptography encryption, offering a fortified shield against potential breaches and unauthorized access.

The primary emphasis is on evaluating the blockchain network's ability to withstand different forms of attack by employing consensus algorithms (Proof of Work (PoW) and Proof of Authority (PoA)). PoW stands out as a superior choice in terms of ensuring the sustained integrity and security of the blockchain network. Even though it necessitates more computational resources and time, its ability to maintain the network's integrity after attacks underscores its reliability and robustness. On the other hand, PoA, while being faster, falls short of ensuring the network's security in the aftermath of attacks, highlighting a significant vulnerability.

Chapter 6

Proposed RL-LEACH

The history of learning models, especially as they relate to machine learning, includes the emergence of numerous methods and strategies that have been employed to help computers learn from data.

• Artificial Intelligence

Artificial Intelligence is the creation of computer programs that can carry out tasks that normally require human intelligence. These activities include speech recognition, visual perception, decision-making, and language translation, among others. The goal of artificial intelligence (AI) is to build devices or systems that can mimic human intelligence and change with the times. Rule-based systems characterized AI and machine learning in their early stages. A set of guidelines for these systems to abide by was specifically programmed into them. These were capable of carrying out certain jobs but were not flexible or able to gain knowledge from experience.

• Machine Learning

A branch of artificial intelligence called machine learning (ML) focuses on creating statistical models and algorithms that let computers carry out tasks without explicit programming. Allowing computers to learn from experience and become more proficient at a given activity or collection of tasks without having to be explicitly programmed for every situation is the main objective of machine learning.

• Deep Learning

A branch of machine learning called "deep learning" is devoted to creating and using artificial neural networks, especially deep neural networks. With layers of networked nodes (neurons) that process information, deep learning models are made to mimic how the human brain functions.

• Reinforcement Learning

Reinforcement Learning (RL) stands at the forefront of advanced machine learning techniques, driving significant progress in artificial intelligence. It is distinguished by its unique approach, where an agent learns to make decisions by interacting with an environment and receiving feedback in the form of rewards or penalties. This learning paradigm mimics the fundamental principles of how humans and animals learn from their experiences, making it exceptionally relevant and adaptable to a wide range of applications, from robotics to game theory.

Figure 6.1 shows how Artificial Intelligence, Machine Learning, Deep Learning, and Reinforcement Learning are interconnected with each other.

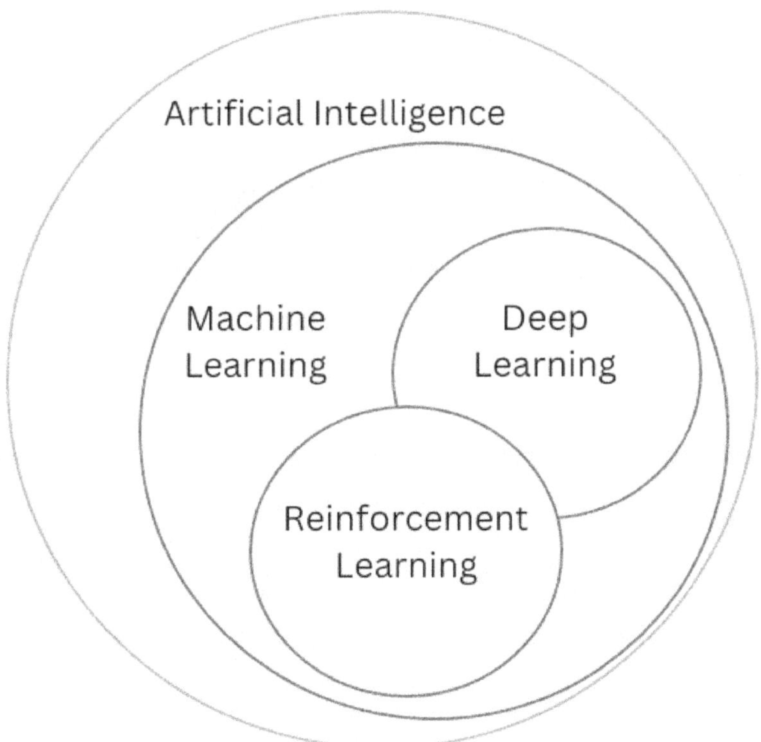

Figure 6.1: AI, ML, DL, RL

The Q-learning algorithm forms the focal point of the exploration, a cornerstone in the field of RL. Q-learning is particularly renowned for its model-free property, allowing agents to learn without a predefined model of the environment. This makes it incredibly versatile and applicable to situations where the dynamics of the environment are complex or unknown. The off-policy nature of Q-learning further enhances its appeal, as it permits the agent to learn from actions that are outside its current policy, thereby broadening its learning scope.

The study delves into the mathematical underpinnings of the Q-learning algorithm, presenting a detailed and structured approach to its implementation. By meticulously defining the algorithm's components, such as the state and action sets, reward function, and the Q-function, a foundation is laid to foster a comprehensive understanding of the workings of Q-learning The iterative process of updating the Q-function based on immediate rewards and future reward estimates forms the crux of the discussion, highlighting the algorithm's capability to balance immediate and long-term rewards effectively.

The potential applications of this RL algorithm are vast and diverse. From optimizing decision-making processes in autonomous systems to enhancing strategies in complex games, the implications of the study are far-reaching. By providing a clear, mathematical formulation of the Q-learning algorithm, the objective is to make a contribution to the growing body of knowledge in RL and offer a resource for researchers and practitioners seeking to apply these concepts in various real-world scenarios.
Mainly three parameters are represented by RL:

a. State

State directly or indirectly affects the action that will be performed by the agent in a particular environment. State in WSN is the information about sensors whether the node is alive or not, the node's residual energy, connectivity status, previous data transmission status, etc.

b. Action

Agents need to take appropriate and optimal actions to maximize the reward. In routing, the selection of the next hop to transmit data is the action that an agent needs to perform in WSN.

c. Reward

Agents take actions according to the states in WSN. The reward is progress in terms of distance towards the destination. Maximizing the reward means to put the step towards the destination node and hence, it enhances the network performance.

Once the file is recovered through the blockchain's PoW algorithm, it is saved in .mat format and proceeds to the training phase of the work. Reinforcement Learning is the technique where decisions are made by taking actions in a particular state and trying to maximize the reward based on output. Here, sensors act as agents and these agents are required to make a selection of paths to deliver data from source to destination to optimize results such as reducing transmission cost and minimizing energy consumption.

In Figure 6.2, a depiction of a Reinforcement Learning model is presented. This model showcases a dynamic system that actively observes and learns from its interactions, aiming to determine optimal actions for transitioning between states. The primary objective of this Reinforcement Learning model is to maximize the cumulative reward it receives over time, achieved through the continuous optimization of its behaviors. In the context of reinforcement learning, the system that is seen here continuously modifies its behavior in response to immediate input from its surroundings. Through adaptive learning, the system can make decisions that result in favorable outcomes and, ultimately, higher total rewards. The picture highlights the dynamic and developing character of the system as it improves its decision-making processes throughout subsequent phases, providing a visual representation of this iterative learning journey.

To put it simply, the Reinforcement Learning model shown in Figure 6.2 represents a self-improving mechanism in which the system continuously learns, modifies, and improves its behavior to maximize cumulative rewards over time.

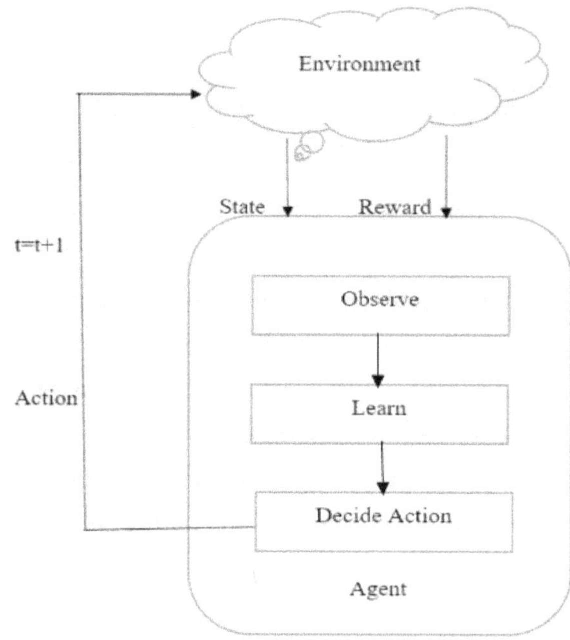

Figure 6.2: A RL Model

6.1 Q-Learning Implementation

Python is utilized to implement a Q-learning algorithm to train a routing protocol in a network with a specified number of nodes. Various parameters such as a number of nodes, gamma, and alpha are defined to configure the Q-learning process. The states, actions, and rewards are set up as arrays and matrices to represent the possible states and actions in the network, as well as the rewards associated with state-action pairs. Q-learning data (data set recovered from PoW) is loaded from a MATLAB file, which contains a matrix (Q) representing Q-values from a previously trained model.

Then a new Q-table is initialized specifically for the routing protocol. Additionally, a matrix is generated to represent the cost of transmission between nodes, providing a basis for evaluating the efficiency of different routing decisions.

The training process is carried out over a specified number of episodes. For each episode, a random initial state is selected, and the Q-learning algorithm updates the Q-values for state-action pairs in the routing protocol Q-table. The training loop continues until reaching the base station or exceeding the maximum number of steps.

Q-learning update rule-

$$Q(s,a)=(1-\alpha).Q(s,a)+\alpha.(R(s,a)-transmission\_cost(s,a)+\gamma.max_{a'}(Q(s',a')))$$

where

•Q(s, a) is the Q-value for current state s and action a.

•α is the learning rate.

•γ is the discount factor.

•R(s, a) is the reward for the current state-action pair.

•transmission_cost(s, a) is the transmission cost for the current state-action pair.

•$max_{a'}$ is maximum over all possible actions in the next state s'.

•Q(s', a') represents the Q-value for the next state s' and action a'.

Using the Q-learning formula, the Q-values are updated during the training phase. This entails considering the factors: the present situation, the action performed, the reward obtained, and the highest Q-value linked to the action that follows. After every episode, the Q-table for the routing protocol is changed, providing a concrete illustration of how the learning process develops and changes.

An invaluable tool that sheds light on the trained routing protocol's developing tactics and decision-making abilities is the updated Q-table. The protocol can learn from its mistakes and become more adept at selecting the best course of action based on observable rewards and environmental conditions thanks to this iterative process. As a culmination of the training phase, the Q-table associated with the trained routing protocol is saved to a MATLAB file. This archival step ensures that the learned knowledge and optimized decision-making policies can be preserved for potential future use or in-depth analysis.

Algorithm: To Perform Training

i. **BEGIN**

ii. Set number of nodes

iii. Set learning parameters α (Learning rate) and γ (Discount factor)

iv. Load Q-Learning data from .mat file and initialize Q-table with zeroes

v. Define transmission cost, number of episodes and maximum steps
vi. Randomly choose the initial state
vii. **FOR** r=1 to r_{max} **DO**
viii. Perform operations:
    a. check state
    b. choose action with highest Q-value for current state
    c. get reward for current state-action pair
ix. Update Q-value for current state action pair
x. **END FOR**
xi. Display updated Q-table
xii. Save trained routing protocol as .mat file
xiii.**END**

A Reinforcement Learning model's training process flow is shown in Figure 6.3. The recovered dataset is loaded and all parameters are initialized to start the process. The transmission cost is then calculated and the Q-table is initialized. The following actions are carried out repeatedly till the episodes are finished:

⇛ Choose the initial state

⇛ If Current state = Base station state

- Choose the action with the highest Q-value.
- Calculate the reward associated with the chosen action.

⇛ Display Q-table after each episode.

Until the target number of episodes is reached, this iterative procedure is carried out. After training is finished, the routing protocol is saved in a .mat file for later usage. An overview of the main procedures for training the Reinforcement Learning model for the routing protocol is shown in the flowchart, which highlights the sequential nature of the Q-table updating, reward computation, state-action selection, and parameter initialization throughout the training episodes.

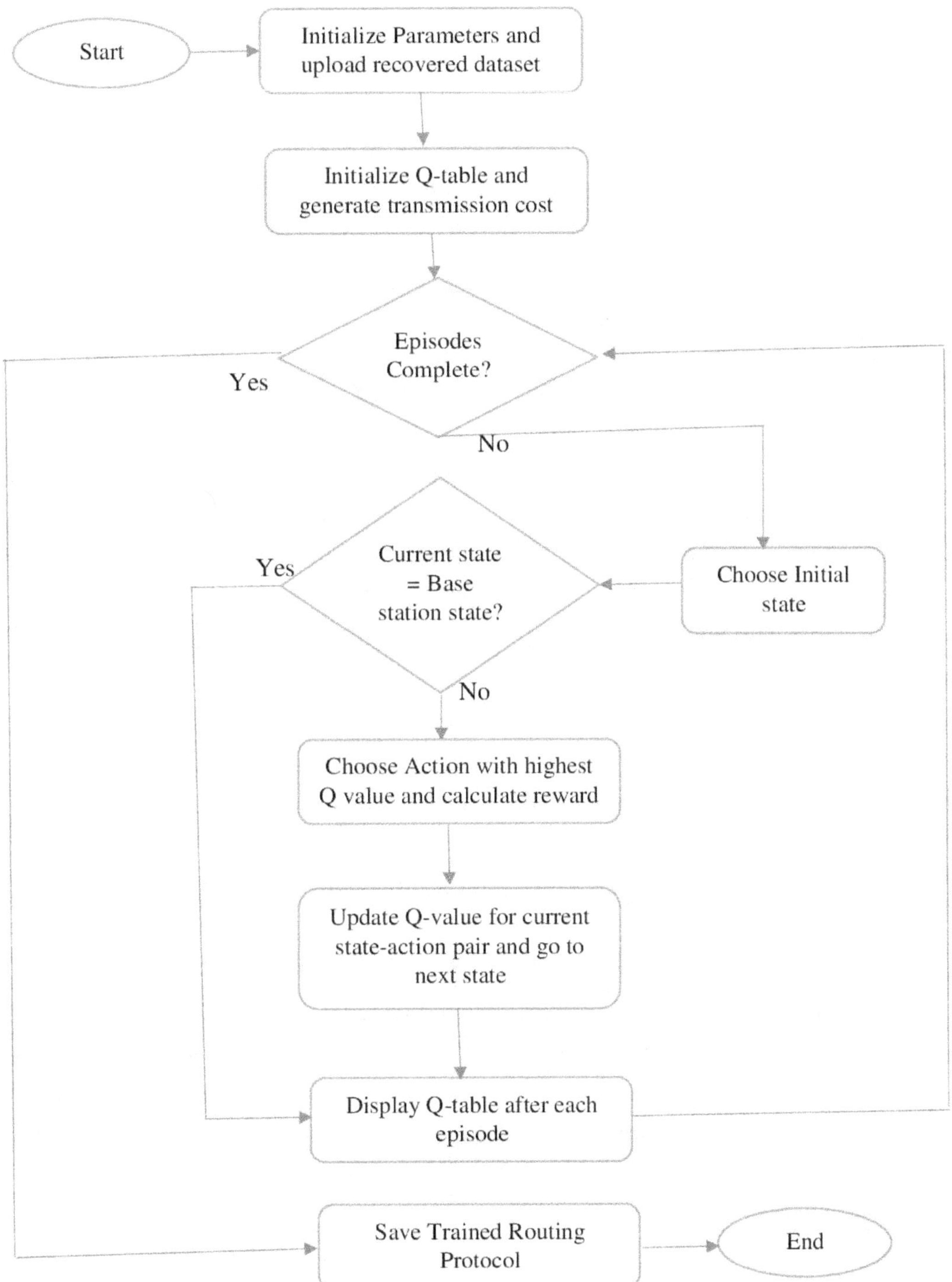

Figure 6.3: Flowchart to Perform Training

6.2 RL-LEACH Implementation

After saving the trained model on blockchain, the transition returns to MATLAB, to develop the proposed RL-LEACH protocol. Low Energy Adaptive Clustering Hierarchy (LEACH) protocol is a technique where the whole network is divided into clusters and a random node in each cluster acts as cluster head. Reinforcement Learning is incorporated with LEACH to perform data transmission efficiently.

6.2.1 Clustering

RL-LEACH is developed for a wireless sensor network (WSN) using a combination of LEACH (Low-Energy Adaptive Clustering Hierarchy) and Q-learning for routing decisions. Firstly, all the parameters related to nodes, environment, cluster heads, energy, etc need to be initialized. To set up a virtual WSN having normal nodes and sink nodes. Afterward, the Q-table is initialized with zeros for all nodes and actions to use it for the Q-learning algorithm in order to make routing decisions. Here, learning rate (alpha) and discount factor (gamma) are established for Q-learning.

A specific proportion of nodes (p) are qualified to become cluster heads in each round (r). This percentage is determined by p and the round number. Nodes use a probabilistic method to determine whether to become cluster heads or not. The amount of energy left in a node affects its likelihood of becoming the cluster head. A node upgrades its type to 'C' (cluster head) and carries out related computations if it chooses to become a cluster head.

After holding their places, the cluster head nodes (C) create clusters around them. Non-clustered nodes (N) link with the closest cluster head, determining the distance and modifying their energy levels correspondingly. The distance between nodes and the type of communication, direct transmission to the base station or transmission to a cluster head, are taken into account when calculating energy usage.

The Q-learning method adjusts the Q-values for every node according to its current state, action, and reward (cost). The node's energy and distance are used to compute the cost. Dead nodes are those whose energy levels fall below a predetermined level. The clustering process is repeated for a predefined number of rounds.

The probability of becoming a cluster head is determined by the following formula:
(p / (1 - p * mod(r, round(1 / p)))) * (S(i).E / Eo)
where
r is the current round.
p is the probability of a sensor node becoming a cluster head.
S(i).E is the current energy of the sensor node.
Eo is initial energy.

Then, for each normal node that is alive and has energy, the Q-learning algorithm is used to update the Q-values based on the current state, action taken, and the resulting state. The Q-values influence the node's decision on whether to transmit data directly to the sink or to transmit to a cluster head. In the end, various statistics are collected throughout the simulation, including the number of dead nodes, alive nodes, total network energy, average energy per node, number of packets sent to the base station, and packets sent to cluster heads.

Implementation Phase

- **Symbols Used**
- *(xm, ym)*: Network size
- *(sink.x, sink.y)*: Sink node coordinates
- *N*:Number of nodes
- *p*: Percentage of nodes act as cluster heads
- E_0:Initial energy
- *ETX, ERX, Efs, Emp, EDA*:Energy consumption parameters

Algorithm: To Implement RL-LEACH

i. **BEGIN**
ii. Upload parameters from trained routing model
iii. Initialize: *(xm, ym), (sink.x, sink.y), N, p,* E_0, *ETX, ERX, Efs, Emp, EDA*
iv. Node setup:
  a. Initial position

b. Energy levels

v. **FOR** r=1 to r_{max} **DO**

vi. Perform operations:

a. form new clusters

b. determine whether node is dead or alive

vii. **END FOR**

viii. **Select Cluster head** based on probabilistic model

ix. **Data Transmission:**

a. Nodes transmit data based on distance and energy considerations.

b. Energy Consumption calculated based on distance.

x. **Update Q-table** based on the cost (distance and energy)

xi. **Statistics collection** (after each round):

a. Dead nodes

b. Alive nodes

c. Network energy

d. Average energy

e. Number of packets transmitted

xii. **END**

In Figure 6.4, the flowchart initiates with the initialization of parameters, nodes, and the sink. The primary function iterates through each round, encompassing steps to ascertain cluster head selection, update information regarding dead nodes, and calculate energy levels within the system.

The main function iterates through each round to check cluster head selection, update dead nodes, and calculate energy levels. The code section identifies the first and tenth dead nodes and determines whether or not all of the network's nodes have stopped functioning. Throughout the procedure, statistics that are essential to comprehending system dynamics are updated regularly. Counts of live nodes, total energy, and cluster heads are a few examples of these metrics.

An essential part of the iterative process is the Q-learning component. Q-values are updated dynamically in response to the current state, the state that emerges from it, and the benefits that result from the activities performed. The mechanism of adaptive learning aids in the system's capacity to improve its decision-making techniques over time.

The whole loop keeps running until the maximum number of rounds that are permitted is reached. After everything is finished, the last statistics are gathered, giving an extensive picture of the system's functionality and information regarding dead nodes.

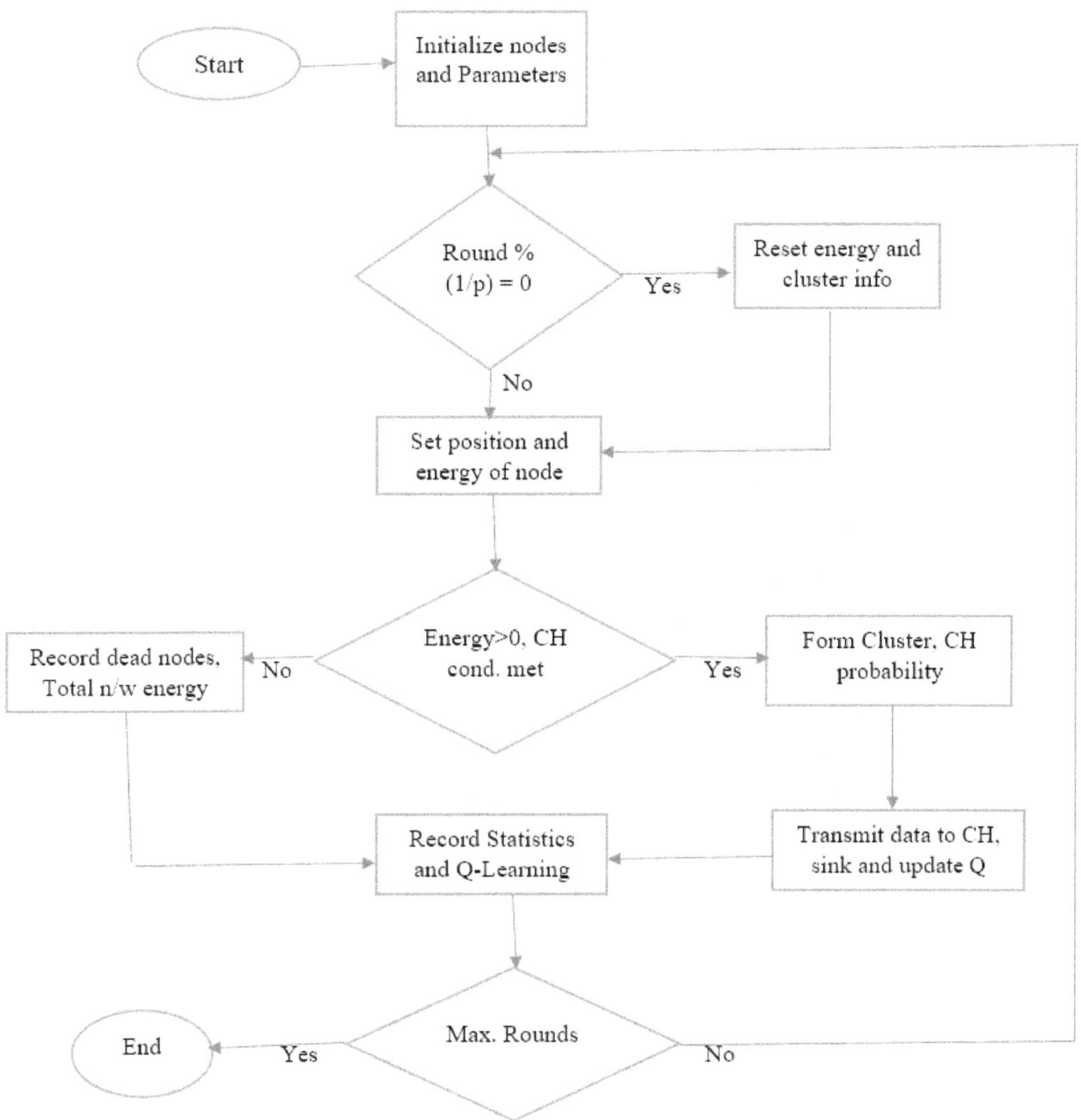

Figure 6.4: Flow Chart of RL-LEACH

To create a complete algorithm for the methodology described in this research, it's essential to integrate the various components involved, including the initialization of the Wireless Sensor Network (WSN) using the RL-LEACH protocol, the integration of blockchain technology for security, and the reinforcement learning process for optimizing network performance. Here's a comprehensive algorithm that encapsulates these elements:

Algorithm: Enhanced WSN Using Blockchain-Based RL-LEACH Protocol

Step I. Initialization

i. **Initialize WSN Parameters**:

a. Define the total number of sensor nodes, N.

b. Set initial energy, E_0, for each node.

c. Initialize no. of rounds, transmission range, and sink node location.

ii. **Blockchain Setup**:

a. Initialize blockchain with SHA256 encryption.

b. Configure blockchain parameters.

c. Implement Proof of Work and Proof of Authority.

iii. **RL-LEACH Protocol Setup**:

a. For each round r in R:

· Elect Cluster Heads (CHs) based on the probabilistic threshold.

Step II. Data Collection and Transmission:

iv. **Data Collection**:

a. Sensor nodes collect environmental data.

v. **Data Transmission and Aggregation**:

a. Sensor nodes transmit data to their respective CHs.

b. CHs aggregate data and transmit it to the base station.

Step III. Reinforcement Learning Integration:

vi. **Reinforcement Learning for Path Optimization**:

a. Implement Q-learning for route optimization:

b. Each node i updates its Q-value.

c. Update rule: $Q(s,a) \leftarrow (1-\alpha).Q(s,a)+\alpha[r+\gamma.\max_{a'}Q(s',a')]$.

Step IV. Security Enhancement through Blockchain:

vii. **Record Transactions in Blockchain**:
   a. Log data transmissions and CH elections in the blockchain.
   b. Validate transactions using the chosen consensus mechanism.

Step V. Performance Evaluation:

viii. **Monitor Network Performance**:
   a. Track metrics like node energy, packets sent etc.

ix. **Policy Improvement and Adaptation**:
   a. Adjust RL-LEACH parameters for future rounds.

Step VI. Termination

x. **End Process**:
   a. Conclusion after all rounds or all nodes depletion.

6.3 Performance Metrics

Various metrics are utilized to analyze the results of the proposed RL-LEACH model, including the number of dead nodes, the number of alive nodes, the number of packets sent to the sink node, residual energy, average energy, and throughput. Table 6.1 shows different metrics to analyze the results.

• Number of Dead Nodes in the Network

This measure expresses the number of nodes in the network that have failed or stopped functioning. The assessment takes into account the relationship between the number of dead nodes and the number of rounds, offering information on the dependability of the system.

• Number of Alive Nodes in the Network

This statistic, which indicates the number of nodes still in operation, is essential for assessing the general robustness and health of the network. An analysis conducted throughout multiple iterations provides a dynamic viewpoint on node activity and stability.

• Throughput

Table 6.1: Performance Metrics

Metrics	Description
Number of dead nodes in the network	Number of dead nodes with respect to number of rounds are evaluated
Number of alive nodes in the network	Number of alive nodes with respect to number of rounds are evaluated
Throughput	Number of packets sent to sink node are evaluated with respect to number of rounds
Remaining energy	Remaining energy of the network is evaluated with respect totime
Network Lifetime	Network lifetime can be evaluated when all nodes die in the network
Network Stability Period	First node, tenth node, and all nodes dead comparison with respect to number of rounds

The amount of packets sent to the sink node relative to all of the network's nodes is used to calculate throughput. This measure gives an idea of how well the network manages data flow.

• **Remaining Energy** This statistic provides insight into patterns of energy use by assessing the network's energy levels across time. Understanding the network's efficiency and sustainability requires keeping an eye on the residual energy.

• **Network Lifetime**

The goal of the network lifetime metric is to ascertain how long it will take for every node in the network to go offline. It is an essential indicator of the network's lifetime and sustainability that sheds light on the system's overall resilience. In the end, these metrics are utilized to compare with other models.

Network Stability Period

This metric assesses the stability of the network by comparing instances of the first node, the tenth node, and all nodes becoming inactive. This comparison is made concerning the progression of rounds in the network.

6.4 Key Features of Proposed Work

• **Integration of Reinforcement Learning with WSN**
a) The proposed work starts with the implementation of RL-LEACH (Reinforcement Learning - Low Energy Adaptive Clustering Hierarchy), a novel adaptation of the LEACH protocol, which is widely used in WSNs for efficient data transmission.

b) The key innovation here is the use of reinforcement learning algorithms to enhance LEACH, enabling the network to learn from its environment and make smarter decisions about data routing. This results in more efficient energy usage and longer network lifespans.

• **Creation and Utilization of a Specialized Dataset**
a) During the operation of RL-LEACH, a unique dataset is generated. This dataset contains valuable insights into network behavior, including how data packets are optimally routed through the network under various conditions.

b) This dataset is more than just raw data; it represents the collective learning and adaptation of the network, a critical resource for further improving network performance.

• **Blockchain for Data Security and Integrity**
a) The integration of blockchain technology is a significant leap in ensuring the security and integrity of the dataset.

b) By storing the dataset on a blockchain, it is ensured that this dataset remains tamper-proof and reliable. This is crucial in scenarios where data security and trust are paramount, such as in critical infrastructure or sensitive research.

• **Advanced Reinforcement Learning for Path Prediction**
a) The secure dataset is then employed to train an advanced reinforcement learning algorithm. This step goes beyond traditional network management techniques.

b) The trained algorithm can predict the most efficient paths for data transmission within the WSN, significantly reducing energy consumption and improving the overall performance of the network.

• **Advanced Combination of Technologies**

a) In this work, The combination employed leverages the strengths of each component.

b) The blockchain secures the data, the reinforcement learning algorithm optimizes the network, and the WSN becomes more efficient and reliable as a result. This multi-disciplinary approach is at the cutting edge of current technological trends.

• **Implications and Applications**

a) This novel approach has wide-ranging implications for the future of WSNs, particularly in areas where network integrity and efficiency are critical.

b) Potential applications could include environmental monitoring, smart cities, military communications, and any domain where sensor networks are essential yet vulnerable to inefficiencies or security breaches.

6.5 Conclusion

In this chapter, the fundamental concepts of Artificial Intelligence (AI), illuminating a number of learning algorithms including machine learning (ML), deep learning, and reinforcement learning (RL) are discussed. This preliminary investigation provided an essential basis laying the groundwork for the later emphasis on the use of RL especially with regard to enhancing Wireless Sensor Networks (WSN).

The main goal was to use RL to improve path selection mechanisms in wireless sensor networks (WSNs). The use of carefully chosen datasets for training enabled RL model to learn and adapt dynamically. This paradigm change toward Reinforcement Learning allowed the wireless sensor network to continuously improve its performance in response to changing circumstances.

The incorporation of Reinforcement Learning into the Low Energy Adaptive Clustering Hierarchy (LEACH) protocol was a significant advancement. This integration was a major step forward, guiding WSNs toward a paradigm of self-optimization. By adding intelligence, RL-LEACH allowed the network to adjust and improve itself on its own without depending on fixed configurations.

Performance metrics were rigorously examined to evaluate the efficacy of RL-LEACH. The discussion extends beyond the technical aspects to describe the key features that distinguish the proposed RL-LEACH model.

Chapter 7

Results and Discussion

As already discussed by using blockchain technology, storing routing data over WSN is secured. The next aim is to make the system energy efficient. For this, an RL-LEACH protocol is developed where Reinforcement Learning is incorporated with LEACH. Three protocols are considered to compare these with the proposed RL-LEACH protocol:

• **LEACH**

Low Energy Adaptive Clustering Hierarchy is a hierarchical clustering-based routing protocol designed to reduce energy consumption in WSNs by organizing sensor nodes into clusters and electing cluster heads to perform data aggregation and transmission. Nodes transmit data to either the sink node or their respective cluster heads based on distance and energy considerations. Energy consumption is calculated based on the distance to the receiving node and the transmission model.

• **Centralized LEACH**

In this, the sink node centrally controls the cluster head selection process based on the energy levels of the sensor nodes. It makes some improvements over standard LEACH, such as considering the average energy of the network and incorporating multi-hop data transmission. The sink node centrally selects cluster heads based on a probabilistic model that considers the node's energy level and the average energy of the network. Only nodes with energy levels above the average are eligible to become cluster heads.

Mishra *et al.* [112] simulates LEACH and Centralized LEACH to compare them with LEACH-DE (Distance Energy). They took 200 nodes and 400*400 m^2 area with an initial energy of 1 joule for each node in the WSN. Results of LEACH, LEACH-C, and LEACH-DE show that the proposed RL-LEACH is superior to all three in terms of the number of packets sent to the sink node, dead and alive nodes over time, and residual energy of the system.

• **TSILEACH**

In TSILEACH (Threshold Sensitive Improved LEACH), Cluster heads (CHs) are chosen using a probabilistic method according to the LEACH protocol. Every node in this procedure creates a random number, which it then compares to a preset threshold value. A node is selected as a cluster head only if the number of nodes within a certain distance is greater than a threshold. Multihop packet transmission to the sink node via multiple cluster heads is considered, and the transmission is allowed only if the minimum distance cluster is not zero.

Azzouz *et al.* [17] proposed an Energy-Aware Cluster Head selection protocol with Balanced Fuzzy C-mean Clustering in WSN. They compared their proposed model with LEACH, LEACH-C, and TSILEACH. They took the area of 100*100 m^2 to randomly deploy 200 nodes with an initial energy of 1 joule/node in the network. Results of RL-LEACH with the same parameters surpass Azzouz *et al.* simulated all the protocols in terms of network stability and dead and alive nodes over the number of rounds.

In simulation results, it is clear that the performance of RL-LEACH is a step ahead of other LEACH, LEACH-C, and TSILEACH. In RL-LEACH when 100 nodes and 100*100 m^2 network area are taken, the first and tenth node dies after 1200 rounds and all nodes die after 1600 rounds which is far better than the other three protocols. The total energy of the network is compared with respect to time. All three protocols exhausted near about 1000 rounds whereas the proposed RL-LEACH performed better and kept its energy level up to 1500 rounds. The number of packets sent to the sink node over time in RL-LEACH is compared with all three protocols. Without any doubt, RL-LEACH surpasses the results produced by the other three algorithms. Then, a number of alive nodes and dead nodes are compared with respect to time in all other protocols. It is observed that the number of alive nodes is much higher in RL-LEACH than in the other three (LEACH, LEACH-C, and TSILEACH).

7.1 Network Stability Period

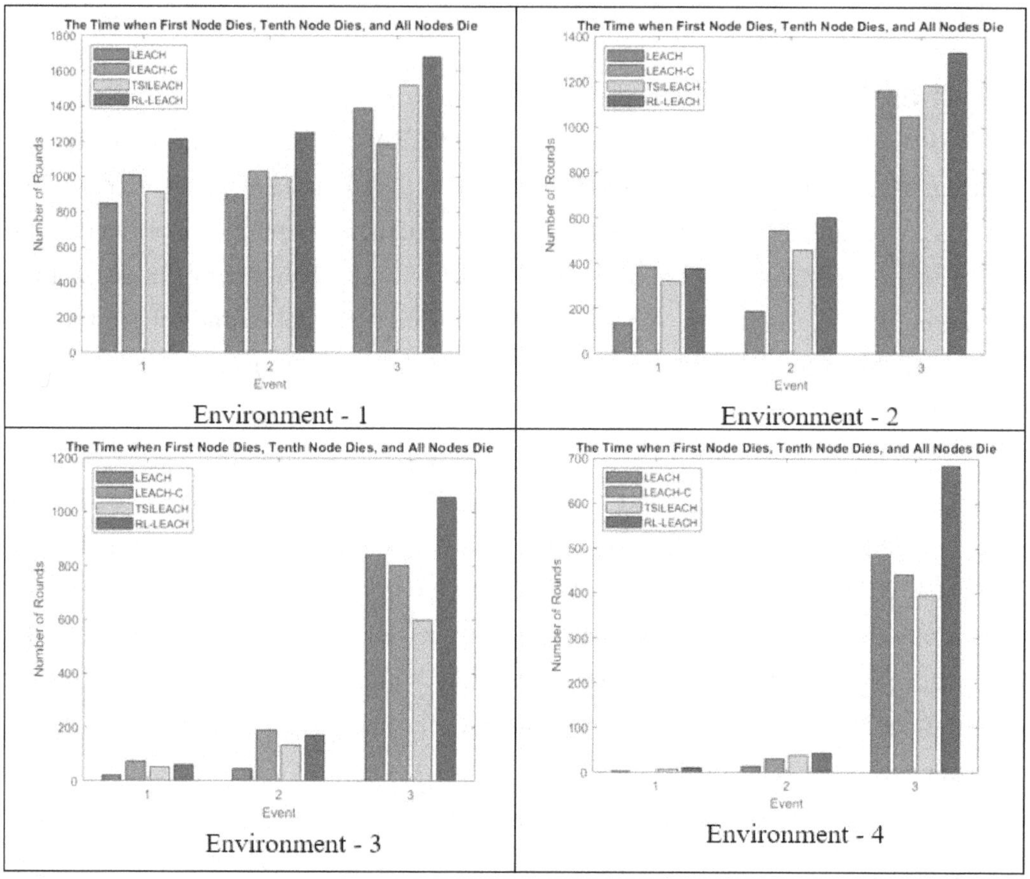

Figure 7.1: Dead Nodes over Number of Rounds

A key component of Wireless Sensor Networks (WSNs) is network stability, which is a measure of the network's effectiveness. The time interval prior to the first node death is the best possible operational condition for the network, with no outages and uninterrupted operation. In Figure 7.1, the simulation results depict the status of 1st node, 10th node, and all nodes being dead over rounds for LEACH, LEACH-C, TSILEACH, and RL-LEACH models in different environments. The bar graphs showcase three events: 1st node, 10th node, and all nodes being dead, represented by blue, red, yellow, and purple colors for LEACH, LEACH-C, TSILEACH, and RL-LEACH, respectively.

In Environment 1, RL-LEACH outperforms other models in all events, with the 1st and 10th nodes lasting until around 1200 rounds, compared to the others failing before 1000 rounds. All nodes are dead after 1600 rounds in RL-LEACH, surpassing LEACH, LEACH-C, and TSILEACH.

Moving to Environment 2, RL-LEACH excels, with the 10th node and all nodes dying after 590 and 1300 rounds respectively, outperforming LEACH, LEACH-C, and TSILEACH. The first node in LEACH-C lasts slightly longer than RL-LEACH. All nodes are dead in 1300 rounds for RL-LEACH, surpassing the other models.

In Environment 3, although LEACH-C performs better when first and 10th node died, RL-LEACH outclasses all models when all nodes are burned, taking 1010 rounds compared to LEACH, LEACH-C, and TSILEACH.

In Environment 4, RL-LEACH outperforms in every event, with the 1st and 10th nodes lasting 12 and 80 rounds, respectively, and all nodes being dead in 450 rounds. This is a superior performance compared to LEACH, LEACH-C, and TSILEACH in the respective events.
Table 7.1 is the tabular representation of the same results as shown in figure 7.1.

Table 7.1: Dead Nodes over Number of Rounds

Env.		**LEACH**	**LEACH-C**	**TSILEACH**	**RL-LEACH**
		Number of Rounds			
Env.: 1	1st node dies	820	1000	850	1200
	10th node dies	830	1000	900	1200
	All nodes die	1300	1100	1400	1600
Env.: 2	1st node dies	150	390	320	380
	10th node dies	175	490	410	590
	All nodes die	1100	990	1110	1300
Env.: 3	1st node dies	20	70	50	60
	10th node dies	20	180	160	170
	All nodes die	800	780	590	1010
Env.: 4	1st node dies	5	1	10	12
	10th node dies	20	40	60	80
	All nodes die	450	420	390	690

7.2 Network Residual Energy

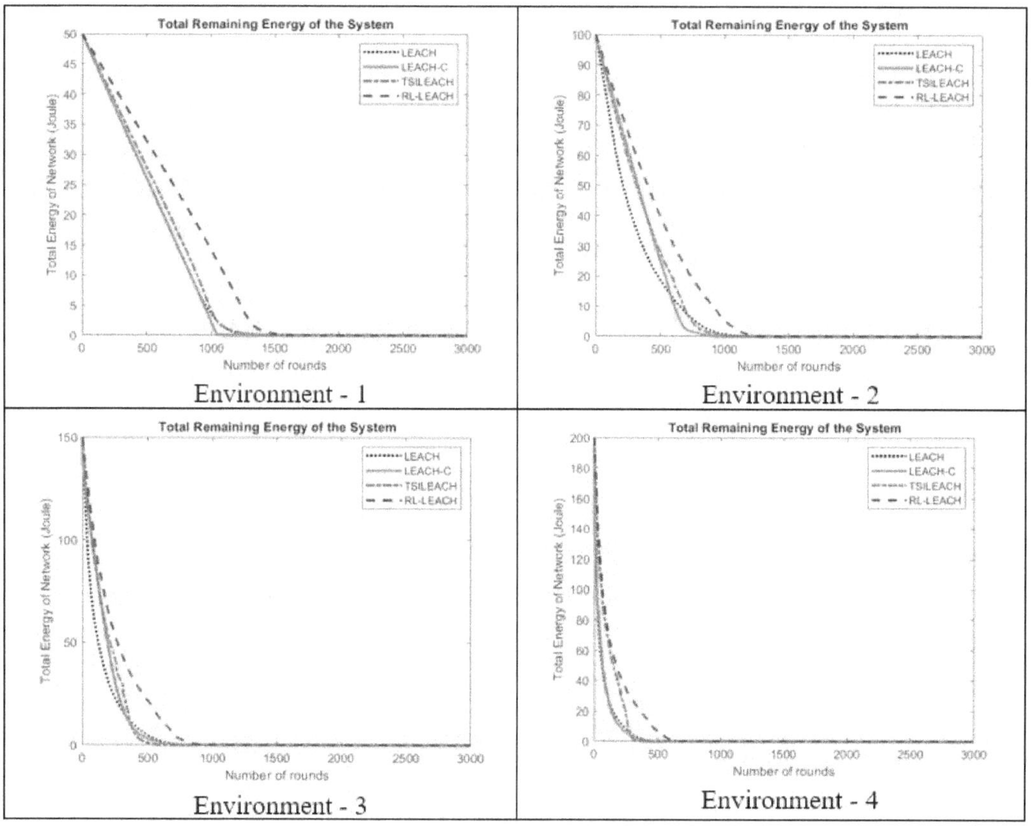

Figure 7.2: Remaining energy of network over number of rounds

Simulation results depicted in Figure 7.2 show the remaining energy of the network over the number of rounds in all four environments. RL-LEACH consistently demonstrated superior energy preservation across different environments, outlasting other models in each scenario and showcasing its effectiveness in prolonging the network's operational lifespan.

In the first round of Environment 1, all models started with an initial energy of 50 J. As the simulation progressed, after 500 rounds, RL-LEACH exhibited remarkable energy preservation with 35 J, outperforming LEACH, LEACH-C, and TSILEACH. By 1000 rounds, RL-LEACH maintained 20 J, showcasing its superior efficiency compared to the other models, which had significantly lower remaining energies (4 J, 1 J, and 5 J for LEACH, LEACH-C, and TSILEACH, respectively).

With an initial energy of 100 J in the first round for all models in Environment 2, RL-LEACH demonstrated exceptional energy conservation. After 500 rounds, RL-LEACH retained 50 J, surpassing LEACH, LEACH-C, and TSILEACH. At 1000 rounds, RL-LEACH maintained 7 J, outperforming the other models that had completely depleted their energy.

Starting with 150 J in the first round for all models in Environment 3, RL-LEACH consistently showcased superior energy management. After 500 rounds, RL-LEACH retained 25 J, while LEACH, LEACH-C, and TSILEACH had significantly lower remaining energies (5 J, 3 J, and 2 J, respectively). Even at 750 rounds, RL-LEACH still had 2 J, outlasting the other models and emphasizing its robust energy preservation capabilities.

In Environment 4, with an initial energy of 200 J in the first round, RL-LEACH consistently outperformed in energy conservation. At 250 rounds, RL-LEACH had 50 J, surpassing LEACH, LEACH-C, and TSILEACH. By 500 rounds, RL-LEACH retained 10 J, while the other models had depleted their energy, underscoring its efficiency in sustaining energy levels over an extended duration.

Table 7.2 serves as a structured representation of the discussed results, presenting the same information covered in the text. This tabular format not only aligns with the preceding discussion but also complements the visual representation offered by Figure 7.2. The integration of numerical data in the table and graphical insights in the figure enhances the comprehensive understanding of the results, providing readers with a multifaceted exploration of the discussed findings.

Table 7.2: Remaining Energy of Network over Number of Rounds

Env.		LEACH	LEACH-C	TSILEACH	RL-LEACH
		Remaining Energy in joules (J)			
Env.: 1	1st Round	50 J	50 J	50 J	50 J
	500 Rounds	25 J	25 J	26 J	35 J
	1000 Rounds	4 J	1 J	5 J	20 J
Env.: 2	1st Round	100 J	100 J	100 J	100 J
	500 Rounds	17 J	25 J	25 J	50 J
	1000 Rounds	0 J	0 J	1 J	7 J
Env.: 3	1st Round	150 J	150 J	150 J	150 J
	500 Rounds	5 J	3 J	2 J	25 J
	750 Rounds	0 J	0 J	0 J	2 J
Env.: 4	1st Round	200 J	200 J	200 J	200 J
	250 Rounds	10 J	10 J	40 J	50 J
	500 Rounds	0 J	0 J	0 J	10 J

7.3 Number of Packets sent

In figure 7.3, the number of packets sent over the number of rounds was illustrated for different environments. RL-LEACH consistently demonstrated superior packet transmission capabilities across various environments, maintaining high efficiency and outperforming other models in terms of the number of packets sent.

In Environment 1, by the 500th round, all models (LEACH, LEACH-C, TSILEACH, and RL-LEACH) transmitted a uniform quantity of packets, totalling 5000. As the simulation advanced to 1500 rounds, RL-LEACH demonstrated efficient packet transmission, dispatching 19,000 packets, surpassing the transmission counts of LEACH, LEACH-C, and TSILEACH, which sent 10,000, 11,000, and 20,000 packets, respectively. This trend persisted at the 3000th round, with RL-LEACH maintaining a robust packet transmission rate of 20,000, showcasing its resilient and effective communication capabilities.

For Environment 2, at the 500th round, RL-LEACH transmitted 8,000 packets, exceeding the transmission rates of LEACH, LEACH-C, and TSILEACH, which sent 7,000, 4,000, and 7,000 packets, respectively. At the 1500th round, RL-LEACH

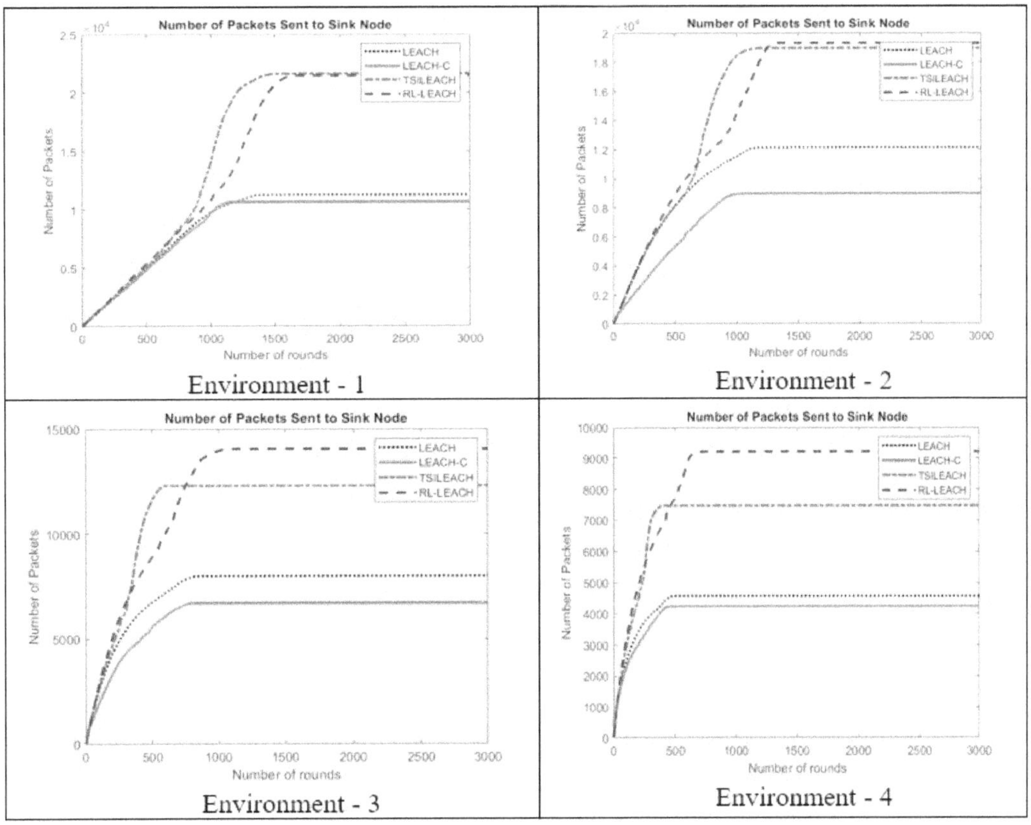

Figure 7.3: Number of Packets Sent over Number of Rounds

sustained its proficient packet transmission, dispatching 19,000 packets, outperforming LEACH, LEACH-C, and TSILEACH, which transmitted 11,000, 8,000, and 18,000 packets, respectively. This effective communication persisted, with RL-LEACH maintaining a consistent packet transmission rate of 19,000 at the 3000th round.

In Environment 3, by the 500th round, RL-LEACH transmitted 9,000 packets, surpassing the transmission rates of LEACH, LEACH-C, and TSILEACH, which sent 6,000, 5,000, and 12,000 packets, respectively. At the 1500th round, RL-LEACH continued its efficient packet transmission, dispatching 14,000 packets, outperforming LEACH, LEACH-C, and TSILEACH, which transmitted 7,500, 6,000, and 12,000 packets, respectively. This sustained effective communication persisted at the 3000th round, with RL-LEACH maintaining a consistent packet transmission rate of 14,000.

Table 7.3: Number of Packets Sent over Number of Rounds

Env.		**LEACH**	**LEACH-C**	**TSILEACH**	**RL-LEACH**
		Number of Packets sent			
Env.: 1	500 Rounds	5000	5000	5000	5000
	1500 Rounds	10000	11000	20000	19000
	3000 Rounds	10000	11000	20000	20000
Env.: 2	500 Rounds	7000	4000	7000	8000
	1500 Rounds	11000	8000	18000	19000
	3000 Rounds	11000	8000	18000	19000
Env.: 3	500 Rounds	6000	5000	12000	9000
	1500 Rounds	7500	6000	12000	14000
	3000 Rounds	7500	6000	12000	14000
Env.: 4	500 Rounds	4200	4000	7200	7500
	1500 Rounds	4200	4000	7200	9200
	3000 Rounds	4000	4000	7200	9200

In the context of Environment 4, by the 500th round, RL-LEACH transmitted 7,500 packets, outshining the transmission rates of LEACH, LEACH-C, and TSILEACH, which sent 4,200, 4,000, and 7,200 packets, respectively. At the 1500th round, RL-LEACH continued its efficient packet transmission, dispatching 9,200 packets, surpassing LEACH, LEACH-C, and TSILEACH, which transmitted 4,200, 4,000, and 7,200 packets, respectively. This reliable communication efficiency was maintained at the 3000th round, with RL-LEACH sustaining a consistent packet transmission rate of 9,200.

Table 7.3 provides an organized display of the results that have been discussed; it presents the same data that have been discussed in the text and illustrated in a related figure 7.3. This tabular style is consistent with the previous explanation and enhances the figure's visual portrayal.

7.4 Network Lifetime in terms of Alive Nodes

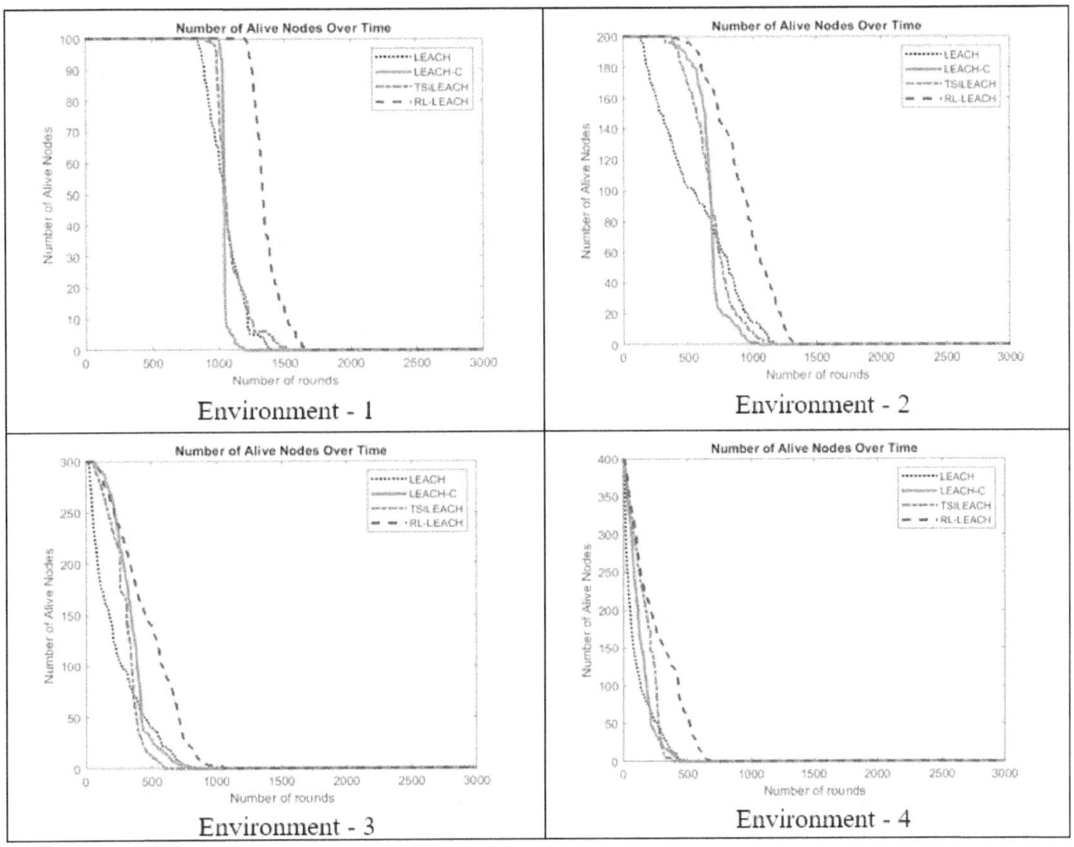

Figure 7.4: Number of Alive Nodes over Number of Rounds

Figure 7.4 highlights the varying effectiveness of the models in terms of node survival across different environments, showcasing RL-LEACH's consistent ability to maintain a higher number of alive nodes.

In the initial round of Environment 1, all models (LEACH, LEACH-C, TSILEACH, and RL-LEACH) commenced with 100 alive nodes. As the simulation progressed to 1000 rounds, the number of alive nodes dwindled to 60 for LEACH, stayed constant at 100 for LEACH-C and RL-LEACH, and dropped to 95 for TSILEACH. By 1500 rounds, LEACH had no remaining alive nodes, LEACH-C and TSILEACH had a minimal presence with 5 and 20 alive nodes, respectively, while RL-LEACH maintained 100 alive nodes, underscoring its resilience and superiority in node survival.

In Environment 2, in the first round, all models began with 200 alive nodes. After 500 rounds, the number of alive nodes decreased to 100 for LEACH, 190 for LEACH-C, 180 for TSILEACH, and remained constant at 200 for RL-LEACH. By 1000 rounds, LEACH had only 20 alive nodes, LEACH-C had none, TSILEACH had 10, and RL-LEACH maintained a robust presence with 80 alive nodes, showcasing its effectiveness in sustaining a larger population of nodes.

In Environment 3, the first round started with 300 alive nodes for all models. After 500 rounds, LEACH had 50 alive nodes, LEACH-C had 30, TSILEACH had 10, and RL-LEACH maintained 150 alive nodes. At 750 rounds, the number of alive nodes further decreased to 20 for LEACH, 10 for LEACH-C, 0 for TSILEACH, and 100 for RL-LEACH. RL-LEACH consistently demonstrated a higher number of surviving nodes throughout the simulation.

For Environment 4, in the initial round, all models began with 400 alive nodes. After 250 rounds, the number of alive nodes decreased to 75 for LEACH, 50 for LEACH-C, 200 for TSILEACH, and 250 for RL-LEACH. By 500 rounds, LEACH and LEACH-C had no remaining alive nodes, TSILEACH had none, and RL-LEACH maintained 50 alive nodes, emphasizing its superior ability to sustain nodes in the network.

Table 7.4 systematically presents the results discussed in the text and illustrated in the corresponding figure 7.4. This tabular format aligns with the previous narrative, ensuring an organized display that augments the visual insights provided in the figure.

Table 7.4: Number of Alive Nodes over Number of Rounds

Env.		**LEACH**	**LEACH-C**	**TSILEACH**	**RL-LEACH**
		Number of Alive nodes			
Env.: 1	1st Round	100	100	100	100
	1000 Rounds	60	100	95	100
	1500 Rounds	0	0	5	20
Env.: 2	1st Round	200	200	200	200
	500 Rounds	100	190	180	200
	1000 Rounds	20	0	10	80
Env.: 3	1st Round	300	300	300	300
	500 Rounds	50	30	10	150
	750 Rounds	20	10	0	100
Env.: 4	1st Round	400	400	400	400
	250 Rounds	75	50	200	250
	500 Rounds	0	0	0	50

7.5 Netwok Lifetime in terms of Dead Nodes

Results in Figure 7.5 indicate the changing number of dead nodes over time for each model in different environments. RL-LEACH consistently exhibited lower numbers of dead nodes compared to other models in various scenarios, highlighting its effectiveness in sustaining the network.

In the initial round of Environment 1, all models (LEACH, LEACH-C, TSILEACH, and RL-LEACH) had zero dead nodes. As the simulation progressed to 1000 rounds, the number of dead nodes increased to 40 for LEACH, remained at zero for LEACH-C, had 5 for TSILEACH, and stayed at zero for RL-LEACH. By 1500 rounds, LEACH had 100 dead nodes, LEACH-C had 100, TSILEACH had 95, and RL-LEACH had 80 dead nodes.

In Environment 2, in the first round, all models had zero dead nodes. After 500 rounds, the number of dead nodes increased to 100 for LEACH, 10 for LEACH-C, 20 for TSILEACH, and remained at zero for RL-LEACH. By 1000 rounds, LEACH had 180 dead nodes, LEACH-C had 200, TSILEACH had 190, and RL-LEACH had

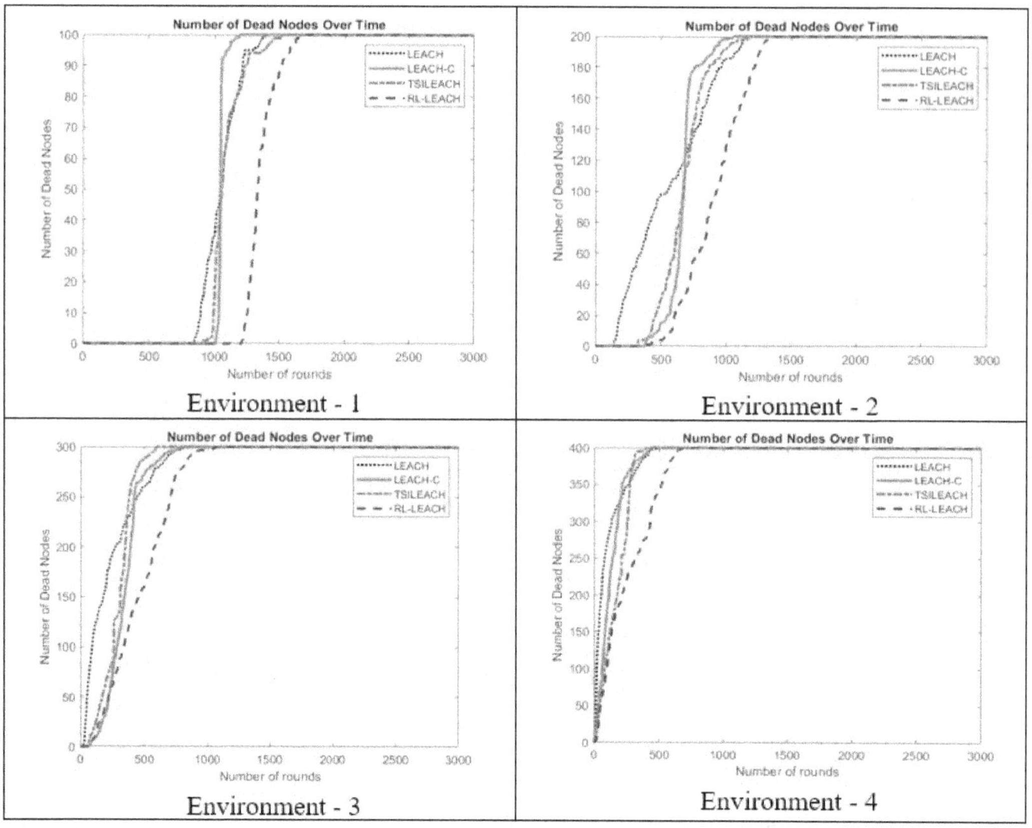

Figure 7.5: Number of Dead nodes over Number of Rounds

120 dead nodes.

In Environment 3, the first round started with all models having zero dead nodes. After 500 rounds, the number of dead nodes increased to 250 for LEACH, 280 for LEACH-C, 290 for TSILEACH, and remained at zero for RL-LEACH. At 750 rounds, the number of dead nodes further increased to 280 for LEACH, 290 for LEACH-C, 300 for TSILEACH, and 200 for RL-LEACH.

For Environment 4, in the initial round, all models had zero dead nodes. After 250 rounds, the number of dead nodes increased to 325 for LEACH, 350 for LEACH-C, 200 for TSILEACH, and 150 for RL-LEACH. By 500 rounds, LEACH had 400 dead nodes, LEACH-C had 400, TSILEACH had 400, and RL-LEACH had 350 dead nodes.

Table 7.5 serves as a methodical showcase of the results deliberated in the text and visually depicted in the linked figure 7.5.

Table 7.5: Number of Dead nodes over Number of Rounds

Env.		LEACH	LEACH-C	TSILEACH	RL-LEACH
		Number of Dead nodes			
Env.: 1	1st Round	0	0	0	0
	1000 Rounds	40	0	5	0
	1500 Rounds	100	100	95	80
Env.: 2	1st Round	0	0	0	0
	500 Rounds	100	10	20	0
	1000 Rounds	180	200	190	120
Env.: 3	1st Round	0	0	0	0
	500 Rounds	250	280	290	150
	750 Rounds	280	290	300	200
Env.: 4	1st Round	0	0	0	0
	250 Rounds	325	350	200	150
	500 Rounds	400	400	400	350

7.6 Conclusion

To sum up, the proposed RL-LEACH is compared with traditional algorithms i.e. LEACH, LEACH-C, and TSILEACH. The evaluation is conducted across several crucial specifications:

- Network Stability Period
- Network Residual Energy
- Number of packets sent to sink node
- Network Lifetime in terms of Alive Nodes
- Network Lifetime in terms of Dead Nodes

When all the components are considered, RL-LEACH emerges as the superior solution when benchmarked against traditional algorithms. It shows overall superiority over LEACH, LEACH-C, and TSILEACH. Reinforcement learning's revolutionary potential for optimizing wireless sensor networks is demonstrated by its combination with the LEACH protocol which provides an appealing option for long-lasting and effective wireless communication systems.

Chapter 8

Conclusion and Future Scope

The study presents a novel blockchain-based architecture intended to improve Wireless Sensor Networks' (WSNs') security and energy efficiency. The research simulates different assaults on a blockchain-based WSN to choose a suitable consensus mechanism with an emphasis on security considerations. A temporary dataset created by a MATLAB-implemented Q-Learning technique is used for these simulations.

Critical network information, including node states, actions, environmental conditions, and transmission paths, are all included in the collection. This dataset is then posted to the blockchain to mimic network attacks. Using a Q-Learning technique guarantees that the dataset includes all relevant facets of the network's activity.

In particular, the study assesses how well two consensus mechanisms—Proof of Work (PoW) and Proof of Authority (PoA)—protect the WSN from various kinds of attacks. Through the use of different consensus processes, the research hopes to learn more about the advantages and disadvantages of each in the context of WSN security. The comparative analysis and simulation results add to a thorough knowledge of PoW and PoA's robustness and performance in the context of safeguarding blockchain-based WSNs.

Following a careful examination, Proof of Work (PoW) is revealed as a consensus method that provides strong security assurances for the blockchain. PoW does this by guaranteeing the blockchain's validity, integrity, and resilience—making it a resilient option against a variety of threats. Notably, PoW strengthens the overall security posture by introducing a recovery mechanism intended to undo the effects of attacks.

Even with its strong security features, PoW has several drawbacks. One important factor to take into account is that, in comparison to Proof of Authority (PoA), an alternative consensus process, this one requires more computer resources and time. Because PoW requires a lot of resources, it might not be the best option in every situation. As such, it becomes crucial to carefully analyze certain use cases and needs when choosing a consensus mechanism.

Assuming that no data loss happened during the simulated attacks, the recoverable data is saved in .mat format when the file is successfully recovered using the blockchain's Proof of Work (PoW) method. The study then moves on to the training stage, where Wireless Sensor Networks (WSNs) are made more energy-efficient through the use of Reinforcement Learning (RL).

During the training phase, individual sensors act as agents, actively choosing paths to optimize various outcomes, such as minimizing energy consumption and lowering transmission costs. In particular, the Q-learning technique is employed by the proposed RL-LEACH algorithm to improve path selection, with the ultimate goal of increasing the WSN's total energy efficiency.

The main objective of the proposed work is to develop and evaluate a blockchain-based model combined with reinforcement learning (RL) for enhancing the security and energy efficiency of wireless sensor networks (WSNs). Two different consensus mechanisms, Proof of Authority (PoA) and Proof of Work (PoW), were implemented and analyzed.

• **Key Findings:**

Performance Metrics:

• Block Creation Time:

PoA demonstrated a significantly lower block creation time of 0.5 seconds compared to PoW's 10 minutes.

• Network Latency:

PoA achieved an average network latency of 0.1 seconds, which is much lower than PoW's 5 seconds.

• Energy Consumption:
PoA showed low energy consumption due to the absence of computational mining, whereas PoW had high energy consumption due to intensive mining processes.

• Throughput:
PoA achieved a high throughput of 1000 transactions per second, while PoW managed only 5 transactions per second.

Security Measures:
• Resistance to Attacks:
PoA was found to be more vulnerable to centralization risks and attacks. However, mechanisms were implemented to detect and respond to these attacks.
PoW demonstrated high resilience against attacks and ensured high integrity due to its decentralized nature and computational difficulty.

Practical Implications:
• Efficiency:
PoA is suitable for applications requiring low latency and high throughput, such as real-time monitoring systems.

• Security:
PoW is ideal for environments where high security and decentralization are critical, despite the trade-offs in energy efficiency and transaction speed.

To confirm and validate our proposed model's superiority over other cutting-edge methods in the field, a thorough comparison is needed. The goal is to show that, in terms of important performance measures, our RL-LEACH method performs better than any other model under consideration. The study compares the outcomes of the RL-LEACH algorithm with those from conventional protocols like LEACH,

TSILEACH, and centralized LEACH to assess the algorithm's efficacy. In the context of energy-efficient routing within WSNs, this comparative analysis aims to illustrate the possible benefits and performance improvements brought about by the RL-LEACH algorithm. The comparisons' outcomes provide important new information about the feasibility and superiority of the proposed RL-LEACH algorithm over traditional protocols for WSN energy optimization and transmission cost reduction. The research takes into account multiple factors, including effectiveness, precision, and flexibility, guaranteeing that our model performs well under a variety of conditions. Establishing RL-LEACH's legitimacy and competitiveness in the context of maximizing energy efficiency in Wireless Sensor Networks (WSNs) is the goal.

8.1 Future Scope

Looking ahead, the future scope of integrating blockchain technology with the RL-LEACH protocol in WSNs is expansive. Potential areas for further exploration include advancements in blockchain integration, and exploring more efficient consensus mechanisms like Proof of Stake (PoS) or Delegated Proof of Stake (DPoS) for scalability and energy efficiency. Incorporating smart contracts could automate network operations while optimizing the RL-LEACH protocol using advanced machine learning algorithms or real-time adaptive strategies could enhance energy efficiency. Integrating energy-harvesting techniques and robust cryptographic methods within the blockchain framework can further improve sustainability and security. Customizing the framework for specific applications such as healthcare, environmental monitoring, smart cities, and industrial IoT offers vast potential. Extending the framework's capabilities to seamlessly integrate with IoT ecosystems and edge computing platforms presents an exciting prospect for more efficient data processing at the network's edge.

Moreover, based on the findings of this study, several potential avenues for future research can be identified to further enhance the integration of blockchain and reinforcement learning (RL) in wireless sensor networks (WSNs):

• **Hybrid Consensus Mechanisms:**

• Combining PoA and PoW: Explore hybrid models that leverage the low latency and energy efficiency of PoA while incorporating the security and decentralization benefits of PoW. Such models could dynamically switch between PoA and PoW based on network conditions and security requirements.
• Adaptive Consensus Algorithms: Develop adaptive algorithms that can modify the consensus mechanism in real-time to optimize performance and security based on the current state of the network.

• **Enhanced Security Protocols:**
• Advanced Attack Detection: Implement more sophisticated techniques for detecting and mitigating attacks, such as machine learning algorithms that analyze network traffic patterns to identify malicious behavior.
• Quantum-Resistant Cryptography: Investigate the use of quantum-resistant cryptographic techniques to future-proof the blockchain against potential threats posed by quantum computing advancements.

• **Scalability Solutions:**
• Sharding and Sidechains: Explore sharding techniques and the use of sidechains to improve the scalability of blockchain networks. This could involve partitioning the network into smaller shards or utilizing sidechains to handle specific tasks, thereby reducing the load on the main blockchain.
• Layer 2 Solutions: Implement Layer 2 solutions like state channels or plasma chains to increase transaction throughput and reduce latency without compromising security.

• **Energy Efficiency Improvements:**
• Green Blockchain Technologies: Investigate alternative, more energy-efficient blockchain technologies and consensus mechanisms. For instance, Proof of Stake (PoS) or Delegated Proof of Stake (DPoS) could be explored as alternatives to PoW.
• Energy Harvesting: Integrate energy harvesting techniques with blockchain nodes to mitigate the high energy consumption associated with PoW. This could involve using renewable energy sources to power the nodes.

• **Integration with Emerging Technologies:**

• Internet of Things (IoT): Further study the integration of blockchain and RL with IoT devices, focusing on secure and efficient data management, device authentication, and seamless interoperability.
• Edge and Fog Computing: Explore the deployment of blockchain and RL in edge and fog computing environments to reduce latency and improve the efficiency of WSNs. This could involve distributing computational tasks across edge devices and fog nodes.

• Data Privacy and Management:
• Privacy-Preserving Techniques: Develop privacy-preserving data management techniques that ensure data integrity and confidentiality while using blockchain. Techniques like homomorphic encryption and zero-knowledge proofs could be explored.
• Decentralized Storage Solutions: Investigate decentralized storage solutions, such as IPFS (InterPlanetary File System), to enhance data availability and resilience in WSNs.

Bibliography

1. A. F. E. Abadi, S. A. Asghari, M. B. Marvasti, G. Abaei, M. Nabavi, and Y. Savaria, "Rlbeep: Reinforcement-learning-based energy efficient control and routing protocol for wireless sensor networks," *IEEE Access*, vol. 10, pp. 44 123–44 135, 2022.

2. S. Aggarwal and N. Kumar, "Chapter twenty - attacks on blockchain working model.," in *The Blockchain Technology for Secure and Smart Applications across Industry Verticals*, ser. Advances in Computers, S. Aggarwal, N. Kumar, and P. Raj, Eds., vol. 121, Elsevier, 2021, pp. 399–410.

3. K. Ahmed and M. A. Gregory, "Techniques and challenges of data centric storage scheme in wireless sensor network," *Journal of Sensor and Actuator Networks*, vol. 1, no. 1, pp. 59–85, 2012, issn: 2224-2708. [Online]. Available: `https://www.mdpi.com/2224-2708/1/1/59`.

4. J. N. Al-Karaki and A. E. Kamal, "Routing techniques in wireless sensor networks: A survey," *IEEE Wireless Communications*, vol. 11, pp. 6–28, 2004.

5. H. A. A. Al-Rawi, A. N. Ming, and K. L. A. Yau, "Application of reinforcement learning to routing in distributed wireless networks: A review," *Artificial Intelligence Review*, vol. 43, pp. 381–416, 2015.

6. N. K. Al-Shammari, T. H. Syed, and M. B. Syed, "An edge–iot framework and prototype based on blockchain for smart healthcare applications," *Engineering, Technology & Applied Science Research*, vol. 11, pp. 7326–7331, 2021.

7. S. Alasaedy, S. Alraddadi, and A. Owais, "A review on using blockchain in wireless sensor networks," *Journal of Theoretical and Applied Information Technology*, vol. 98, no. 23, 2020.

8. K. H. Ali and A. F. M. S. Shah, "Performance comparison of pegasis, heed, and leach protocols in wireless sensor networks," *Celal Bayar University Journal of Science*, vol. 19, pp. 11–18, 1 2023.

9. S. Ali, G. Wang, M. Z. A. Bhuiyan, and H. Jiang, "Secure data provenance in cloud-centric internet of things via blockchain smart contracts," in *Proceedings of the 2018 IEEE SmartWorld, Ubiquitous Intelligence & Computing, Advanced & Trusted Computing, Scalable Computing & Communications, Cloud & Big Data Computing, Internet of People and Smart City Innovation (SmartWorld/SCALCOM/UIC/ ATC/CBDCom/IOP/SCI)*, Guangzhou, China, 2018, pp. 991–998.

10. E. Alpaydin, *Introduction to Machine Learning* (Adaptive Computation and Machine Learning series). The MIT Press, 2004, p. 400, isbn: 9780262012119.

11. S. Alsaedy, S. Alraddadi, and A. Owais, "A review on using blockchain in wireless sensor networks," *Journal of Theoretical and Applied Information Technology*, vol. 98, no. 23, 2020.

12. S. R. Anand, R. C. Tanguturi, and S. R. D. S, "Blockchain based packet delivery mechanism for wsn," *International Journal of Recent Technology and Engineering (IJRTE)*, vol. 8, no. 2, pp. 2277–3878, 2019.

13. A. Angrish, B. Craver, M. Hasan, and B. Starly, "A case study for blockchain in manufacturing: "fabrec": A prototype for peer-to-peer network of manufacturing nodes," *arXiv preprint arXiv:1804.01083*, 2018.

14. Y. Aoki, K. Otsuki, T. Kaneko, R. Banno, and K. Shudo, "Simblock: A blockchain network simulator," in *IEEE INFOCOM 2019 - IEEE Conference on Computer Communications Workshops (INFOCOM WKSHPS)*, 2019, pp. 325–329.

15. A. Arshad, Z. Mohd Hanapi, S. Subramaniam, and R. Latip, "A survey of sybil attack countermeasures in iot-based wireless sensor networks," *PeerJ. Computer science*, vol. 7, pp. 673–680, 2021, issn: 2376-5992.

16. S. Awan, N. Javaid, S. Ullah, A. U. Khan, A. M. Qamar, and J.-G. Choi, "Blockchain based secure routing and trust management in wireless sensor networks," *Sensors*, vol. 22, no. 2, 2022, issn: 1424-8220.

17. I. Azzouz, B. Boussaid, A. Zouinkhi, and M. Abdelkrim, "Energy-aware cluster head selection protocol with balanced fuzzy c-mean clustering in wsn," in *2022 19th International Multi-Conference on Systems, Signals Devices (SSD)*, 2022, pp. 1534–1539.

18. L. Bach, B. Mihaljevic, and M. Zagar, "Comparative analysis of blockchain consensus algorithms," in *Proceedings of the 2018 IEEE 41st International Convention on Information and Communication Technology, Electronics and Microelectronics (MIPRO)*, Opatija, Croatia, 2018, pp. 1545–1550.

19. P. Bakaraniya and S. Mehta, "K-leach: An improved leach protocol for lifetime improvement in wsn," in *Conference on Information and Knowledge Technology (IKT)*, 2013.

20. A. Banafa, "Iot and blockchain convergence: Benefits and challenges," 2017. [Online]. Available: `https://api.semanticscholar.org/CorpusID:217055419`.

21. Z. Bao, Q. Wang, W. Shi, L. Wang, H. Lei, and B. Chen, "When blockchain meets sgx: An overview, challenges, and open issues," *IEEE Access*, vol. 8, pp. 170 404–170 420, 2020.

22. A. Begum, A. Tareq, M. Sultana, M. Sohel, T. Rahman, A. H. Sarower, and T. Bhuiyan, "Blockchain attacks, analysis and a model to solve double spending attack," Aug. 2019.

23. T. M. Behera and et al., "Energy-efficient routing protocols for wireless sensor networks: Architectures, strategies, and performance," *Electronics*, vol. 11, no. 15, p. 2282, 2022.

24. H. Beniata, A. Anagreh, and A. Kertesz, "Dons: Dynamic optimized neighbor selection for smart blockchain networks," *Future Generation Computer Systems*, vol. 130, pp. 75–90, 2022.

25. S. Bharany and et al., "Energy-efficient clustering scheme for flying ad-hoc networks using an optimized LEACH protocol," *Energies*, vol. 14, no. 19, p. 6016, 2021.

26. K. V. Bhaskar, R. Seshadri, and R. M. Reddy, "Applications and techniques in wireless sensor networks: A survey," *International Journal of Engineering Research and Technology (IJERT)*, 2014, NCDMA – 2014.

27. B. Bhushan and N. Sharma, "Transaction privacy preservations for blockchain technology," in *International Conference on Innovative Computing and Communications*, Singapore: Springer, 2021, pp. 377–393.

28. G. Boateng, D. Ayepah-Mensah, D. Doe, A. Mohammed, G. Sun, and G. Li, "Blockchain-enabled resource trading and deep reinforcement learning-based autonomous ran slicing in 5g," *IEEE Transactions on Network and Service Management*, vol. 19, no. 1, pp. 216–227, 2022.

29. K. Botros, "The role of blockchain in reducing the cost of financial transactions in the retail industry," in *Workshop on Computer Networks & Communications*, vol. 2889, Chennai, India, 2021, p. 2.

30. I. D. Buldin, M. G. Gorodnichev, S. S. Makhrov, and E. N. Denisova, "Next generation industrial blockchain-based wireless sensor networks," in *2018 Wave Electronics and its Application in Information and Telecommunication Systems (WECONF)*, 2018, pp. 1–5.

31. R. Casado-Vara, "Stochastic approach for prediction of wsn accuracy degradation with blockchain technology," in *Distributed Computing and Artificial Intelligence, Special Sessions, 15th International Conference*, 2019, pp. 422–425.

32. F. Casino, T. K. Dasaklis, and C. Patsakis, "A systematic literature review of blockchain-based applications: Current status, classification and open issues," *Telematics and Informatics*, vol. 36, pp. 55–81, 2019.

33. R. Chaganti, B. Bhushan, and V. Ravi, "A survey on blockchain solutions in ddos attacks mitigation: Techniques, open challenges and future directions," *Computer Communications*, vol. 197, pp. 96–112, 2023, issn: 0140-3664.

34. A. Chandra and P. Kansal, "P-leach protocol for wireless sensor network," *INTERNATIONAL JOURNAL FOR RESEARCH IN APPLIED SCIENCE AND ENGINEERING TECHNOLOGY*, 2014.

35. Y. Chen, H. Chen, Y. Zhang, M. Han, M. Siddula, and Z. Cai, "A survey on blockchain systems: Attacks, defenses, and privacy preservation," *High-Confidence Computing*, vol. 2, no. 2, p. 100 048, 2022, issn: 2667-2952.

36. Y.-S. Chen, Y. Ren, Y. Liu, S. Ji, A. K. Sangaiah, and J. Wang, "Incentive mechanism of data storage based on blockchain for wireless sensor networks," *Mobile Information Systems*, vol. 2018, p. 6 874 158, 2018, issn: 1574-017X.

37. Z. Cui, F. Xue, S. Zhang, X. Cai, Y. Cao, W. Zhang, and J. Chen, "A hybrid blockchain-based identity authentication scheme for multi-wsn," *IEEE Transactions on Services Computing*, vol. 13, no. 2, pp. 241–251, 2020.

38. J. Czech, "Distributed methods for reinforcement learning survey," in *Reinforcement Learning Algorithms: Analysis and Applications*. Berlin, Germany: Springer, 2021.

39. I. Daanoune, A. Baghdad, and A. Ballouk, "Improved LEACH protocol for increasing the lifetime of WSNs," *Int. J. Electr. Comput. Eng. (IJECE)*, vol. 11, pp. 3106–3113, 2021.

40. M. Dagar and S. Mahajan, "Data aggregation in wireless sensor network: A survey," *International Journal of Information and Computation Technology*, vol. 3, no. 3, pp. 167–174, 2013, issn: 0974-2239.

41. Q. Dai, B. Zhang, and S. Dong, "Eclipse attack detection for blockchain network layer based on deep feature extraction," *Wireless Communications and Mobile Computing*, vol. 2022, pp. 1–19, Apr. 2022. doi: 10.1155/2022/1451813.

42. P. De Filippi, M. Mannan, and W. Reijers, "Blockchain as a confidence machine: The problem of trust challenges of governance," *Technology in Society*, vol. 62, p. 101 284, 2020, issn: 0160-791X.

43. S. Deshpande, J. Gujarathi, P. Chandre, and P. Nerkar, "A comparative analysis of machine deep learning algorithms for intrusion detection in wsn," in *Security Issues and Privacy Threats in Smart Ubiquitous Computing*. Singapore: Springer, 2011, pp. 173–193.

44. E. Djéné, Y. Frédéric, M. S. E. Idrissi, P.-M. Tardif, A. Jorio, B. E. Bhiri, and Y. Fakhri, "A formal energy consumption analysis to secure cluster-based wsn: A case study of multi-hop clustering algorithm based on spectral classification using lightweight blockchain," *Sensors*, vol. 22, no. 20, p. 7730, 2022.

45. D. Elangovan, C. Long, F. Bakrin, C. Tan, K. Goh, S. Yeoh, M. Loy, Z. Hussain, K. Lee, A. Idris, and L. Ming, "The use of blockchain technology in the health care sector: Systematic review," *JMIR Medical Informatics*, vol. 10, no. 1, e17278, 2022.

46. M. Elshrkawey, H. Al-Mahdi, and W. Atwa, "An enhanced routing algorithm based on a re-position particle swarm optimization (ra-rpso) for wireless sensor network," *Journal of King Saud University - Computer and Information Sciences*, vol. 34, pp. 10 304–10 318, 10, Part B 2022.

47. A.-m. Farahmand, A. Shademan, M. Jagersand, and C. SzepesvÃ¡ri, "Model-based and model-free reinforcement learning for visual servoing," Jun. 2009, pp. 2917 –2924.

48. L. Feng, H. Zhang, L. Lou, and Y. Chen, "A blockchain-based collocation storage architecture for data security process platform of wsn," in *2018 IEEE 22nd International Conference on Computer Supported Cooperative Work in Design ((CSCWD))*, 2018, pp. 75–80.

49. B. Ghaleb, A. Al-Dubai, E. Ekonomou, M. Qasem, I. Romdhani, and L. Mackenzie, "Addressing the dao insider attack in rpl's internet of things networks," *IEEE Communications Letters*, vol. 23, pp. 68–71, 2018.

50. P. Gnanasundari and K. S. S. Rani, "Blockchain assisted node validation approach for security provisioning in wsn environment," *Journal of Intelligent & Fuzzy Systems*, vol. 44, no. 3, pp. 2817–2829, 2023. doi: 10.3233/JIFS-223413.

51. K. Godawatte, P. Branch, and J. But, "Use of blockchain in health sensor networks to secure information integrity and accountability," *Procedia Computer Science*, vol. 210, pp. 124–132, 2022, issn: 1877-0509.

52. A. D. L. R. Gómez-Arevalillo and P. Papadimitratos, "Blockchain-based public key infrastructure for inter-domain secure routing," in *Proceedings of the International Workshop on Open Problems in Network Security (iNetSec)*, Rome, Italy, 2017, pp. 20–38.

53. P. Gou, F. Li, Z. Li, and X. Jia, "Improved LEACH protocol based on efficient clustering in wireless sensor networks," *Journal of Computational Methods in Sciences and Engineering*, vol. 19, no. 3, pp. 827–838, 2019.

54. A. Guerrero-Sanchez, E. Rivas-Araiza, J. Gonzalez-Cordoba, M. Toledano-Ayala, and A. Takacs, "Blockchain mechanism and symmetric encryption in a wireless sensor network," *Sensors*, vol. 20, p. 2798, 2020.

55. S. Gurung, D. Lin, A. Squicciarini, and E. Bertino, "Information-oriented trustworthiness evaluation in vehicular ad-hoc networks," in *Proceedings of the International Conference on Network and System Security*, Springer, Berlin, Germany, 2013, pp. 94–108.

56. J. H and J. K, "T-leach: The method of threshold-based cluster head replacement for wireless sensor networks," *Information Systems Frontiers*, 2008. doi: 10.1007/s10796-008-9121-4.

57. F. Hajjej, M. Hamdi, R. Ejbali, and M. Zaied, "A distributed coverage hole recovery approach based on reinforcement learning for wireless sensor networks," *Ad Hoc Networks*, vol. 101, p. 102 082, 2020. doi: 10.1016/j.adhoc.2019.102082.

58. M. Hamza, A. Hashim, D. Elkamchouchi, N. Nemri, J. Alzahrani, A. Aziz, M. Ibrahim, and A. Motwakel, "Energy-efficient routing using novel optimization with tabu techniques for wireless sensor network," *Computer Systems Science and Engineering*, vol. 45, pp. 1711–1726, Jan. 2023.

59. M. F. Hashmi, T. Sharma, A. Balyan, R. Nair, P. Jain, S. Arora, and F. Ahmadi, "Relec: A reinforcement learning-based clustering-enhanced protocol for efficient energy optimization in wireless sensor networks," *Wireless Communications and Mobile Computing*, vol. 2022, p. 3 337 831, 2022, issn: 1530-8669.

60. W. R. Heinzelman, A. Chandrakasan, and H. Balakrishnan, "Energy-efficient communication protocol for wireless microsensor networks," in *Proceedings of the 33rd Annual Hawaii International Conference on System Sciences*, 2000, 10 pp. vol.2–. doi: 10.1109/HICSS.2000.926982.

61. A. HNINI, A. EZZATI, M. FIHRI, and A. HAJAMI, "W-LEACH Decentralized: Weighted leach with a decentralized way," *IOSR Journal of Computer Engineering (IOSR-JCE)*, 2014.

62. S.-J. Hsiao and W.-T. Sung, "Employing blockchain technology to strengthen security of wireless sensor networks," *IEEE Access*, vol. 9, pp. 72 326–72 341, 2021. doi: `10.1109/ACCESS.2021.3079708`.

63. S.-J. Hsiao and W.-T. Sung, "Utilizing blockchain technology to improve wsn security for sensor data transmission," *Computers, Materials Continua*, vol. 68, pp. 1899–1918, Jan. 2021.

64. H. M. Hussien, S. M. Yasin, S. N. I. Udzir, A. A. Zaidan, and B. B. Zaidan, "A systematic review for enabling of develop a blockchain technology in healthcare application: Taxonomy, substantially analysis, motivations, challenges, recommendations and future direction," *Journal of Medical Systems*, vol. 43, p. 320, 2019.

65. M. J. Islam, A. Rahman, S. Kabir, M. R. Karim, U. K. Acharjee, M. K. Nasir, and S. Wu, "Blockchain-sdn-based energy-aware and distributed secure architecture for iot in smart cities," *IEEE Internet of Things Journal*, vol. 9, no. 5, pp. 3850–3864, 2022.

66. S. Jain and N. Agrawal, "Development of energy efficient modified LEACH protocol for IoT applications," in *2020 12th International Conference on Computational Intelligence and Communication Networks (CICN)*, IEEE, 2020, pp. 160–164.

67. B. Jamal, T. Mona, O. Hadi, and B. Kaveh, "A reinforcement learning model for the reliability of blockchain oracles," *Expert Systems with Applications*, vol. 214, 2023, In Press.

68. F. Jameel, U. Javaid, W. U. Khan, M. N. Aman, H. Pervaiz, and R. Jäntti, "Reinforcement learning in blockchain-enabled iiot networks: A survey of recent advances and open challenges," *Sustainability*, vol. 12, no. 13, p. 5161, 2020. doi: `10.3390/su12135161`.

69. F. Jameel, U. Javaid, W. U. Khan, M. N. Aman, H. Pervaiz, and R. JÃ¤ntti, "Reinforcement learning in blockchain-enabled iiot networks: A survey of recent advances and open challenges," *Sustainability*, vol. 12, no. 12, 2020, issn: 2071-1050.

70. F. Jameel, W. U. Khan, S. T. Shah, and T. Ristaniemi, "Towards intelligent iot networks: Reinforcement learning for reliable backscatter communications," *2019 IEEE Globecom Workshops (GC Wkshps)*, pp. 1–6, 2019.

71. F. Jameel, S. Wyne, G. Kaddoum, and T. Q. Duong, "A comprehensive survey on cooperative relaying and jamming strategies for physical layer security," *IEEE Communications Surveys & Tutorials*, vol. 21, pp. 2734–2771, 2019.

72. D. Javeed, T. Gao, and M. T. Khan, "Sdn-enabled hybrid dl-driven framework for the detection of emerging cyber threats in iot," *Electronics*, vol. 10, no. 8, p. 918, 2021.

73. U. Jayasinghe, G. M. Lee, □. MacDermott, and W. S. Rhee, "Trustchain: A privacy preserving blockchain with edge computing," *Wireless Communications and Mobile Computing*, vol. 2019, pp. 1–17, Jul. 2019.

74. Q. Jiang, S. Zeadally, J. Ma, and D. He, "Lightweight three-factor authentication and key agreement protocol for internet-integrated wireless sensor networks," *IEEE Access*, vol. 5, pp. 3376–3392, 2017.

75. Z. K, M. M, and A. A.A, "Sybil attack detection in wireless sensor networks," Oct. 2020, pp. 1–6.

76. D. Kandris, C. Nakas, D. Vomvas, and G. Koulouras, "Applications of wireless sensor networks: An up-to-date survey," *Appl. Syst. Innov.*, vol. 3, no. 1, p. 14, Feb. 2020.

77. J. Kang, X. Huang, M. Wu, S. Maharjan, S. Xie, and Y. Zhang, "Blockchain for secure and efficient data sharing in vehicular edge computing and networks," *IEEE Internet of Things Journal*, vol. PP, pp. 1–1, Oct. 2018.

78. P. Kaur and E. L. Cha, "An enhanced energy efficient low energy adaptive clustering hierarchy (leach) protocol for wsns," *International Journal of Advanced Research in Computer Science and Software Engineering*, vol. 6, no. 7, 2016.

79. B. Kfoury, "The role of blockchain in reducing the cost of financial transactions in the retail industry," in *Workshop on Computer Networks & Communications*, vol. 2889, Chennai, India, 2021.

80. R. Khalid, M. Malik, T. Alghamdi, and N. Javaid, "A consortium blockchain-based energy trading scheme for electric vehicles in smart cities," *Journal of Information Security and Applications*, vol. 63, p. 102 998, 2021.

81. A. S. Khan, K. Balan, Y. Javed, S. Tarmizi, and J. Abdullah, "Secure trust-based blockchain architecture to prevent attacks in vanet," *Sensors*, vol. 19, no. 22, 2019, issn: 1424-8220.

82. Z. Khan, G. Latif, A. Sher, I. Usman, M. Ashraf, M. Ilahi, and N. Javaid, "Efficient routing for corona based underwater wireless sensor networks," *Computing*, vol. 101, pp. 831–856, 2019.

83. D. S Kim and Y. J Chung, "Self-organization routing protocol supporting mobile nodes for wireless sensor network," in *Proc. First International Multi-Symposiums on Computer and Computational Sciences*, Hangzhou, China, 2006.

84. T.-H. Kim, R. Goyat, M. K. Rai, G. Kumar, W. J. Buchanan, R. Saha, and R. Thomas, "A novel trust evaluation process for secure localization using a decentralized blockchain in wireless sensor networks," *IEEE Access*, vol. 7, pp. 184 133–184 144, 2019.

85. T. Kim, R. Goyat, M. Rai, G. Kumar, W. Buchanan, R. Saha, and R. Thomas, "A novel trust evaluation process for secure localization using a decentralized blockchain in wireless sensor networks," *IEEE Access*, vol. 7, pp. 184 133–184 144, 2019.

86. N. K.P, "Wireless sensor networks – scalability and performance issues: A review," *International Journal of Computer Science and Technology (IJCST)*, vol. 6, no. 1, Page Range, 2015.

87. M. Kumar, P. Mukherjee, S. Verma, Kavita, M. Kaur, S. Singh, M. Kobielnik, M. WoÅºniak, J. Shafi, and M. F. Ijaz, "Bbnsf: Blockchain-based novel secure framework using rp2-rsa and asr-ann technique for iot enabled healthcare systems," *Sensors*, vol. 22, no. 23, 2022, issn: 1424-8220. [Online]. Available: `https://www.mdpi.com/1424-8220/22/23/9448`.

88. N. M. Kumar and P. K. Mallick, "Blockchain technology for security issues and challenges in iot," *Procedia Computer Science*, vol. 132, pp. 1815–1823, 2018.

89. R. Kumar, F. Khan, A. Imoize, J. Ogbebor, S. Kadry, and S. Rho, "Blockchain-based wireless sensor networks for malicious node detection: A survey," *IEEE Access*, vol. PP, pp. 1–1, Sep. 2021.

90. Q. L and Z. H, "An energy balanced clustering algorithm based on leach protocol," in *Proceedings of the 2nd International Conference on Systems Engineering and Modeling (ICSEM-13)*, Paris, France, 2013, pp. 72–73.

91. A. Lakhan, M. A. Mohammed, J. Nedoma, R. Martinek, P. Tiwari, and N. Kumar, "Drlbts: Deep reinforcement learning-aware blockchain-based healthcare system," *Scientific Reports*, vol. 13, no. 1, p. 4124, 2023, issn: 2045-2322.

92. T. H. Law, S. Erol, and L. Tseng, *Longest-chain attacks: Difficulty adjustment and timestamp verifiability*, 2023. arXiv: `2308.15312 [cs.CR]`.

93. H. Lee and K. Ke, "Monitoring of large-area iot sensors using a lora wireless mesh network system: Design and evaluation," *IEEE Transactions on Instrumentation and Measurement*, vol. 67, pp. 2177–2187, 2018.

94. C. ta Li, "Security of wireless sensor networks: Current status and key issues," in *Smart Wireless Sensor Networks*, H. D. Chinh and Y. K. Tan, Eds., Rijeka: IntechOpen, 2010, ch. 17.

95. J. Li, G. Liang, and T. Liu, "A novel multi-link integrated factor algorithm considering node trust degree for blockchain-based communication," *KSII Transactions on Internet and Information Systems*, vol. 11, pp. 3766–3788, Aug. 2017.

96. X. Li, M. R. Lyu, and J. Liu, "A trust model based routing protocol for secure ad hoc networks," in *Proceedings of the 2004 IEEE Aerospace Conference Proceedings (IEEE Cat. No.04TH8720)*, vol. 2, Big Sky, MT, USA, 2004, pp. 1286–1295.

97. X. Li and W. Wu, "Recent advances of blockchain and its applications," *Journal of Social Computing*, vol. 3, no. 4, pp. 363–394, 2022.

98. X. Li, Z. Jia, P. Zhang, R. Zhang, and H. Wang, "Trust-based on-demand multipath routing in mobile ad hoc networks," *IET Inf. Secur.*, vol. 4, pp. 212–232, 2010. [Online]. Available: `https://api.semanticscholar.org/CorpusID:17988886`.

99. X Liang, D Yuzhen, J Donghua, H Jinhao, W Dongming, L Jie, and H. V. Poor, "A reinforcement learning and blockchain-based trust mechanism for edge networks," *IEEE Transactions on Communications*, pp. 1–1, 2020.

100. M. Liu, F. R. Yu, Y. Teng, V. C. Leung, and M. Song, "Performance optimization for blockchain-enabled industrial internet of things (iiot) systems: A deep reinforcement learning approach," *IEEE Transactions on Industrial Informatics*, vol. 15, pp. 3559–3570, 2019.

101. M. Liu, Y. Teng, F. R. Yu, V. C. M. Leung, and M. Song, "Deep reinforcement learning based performance optimization in blockchain-enabled internet of vehicle," in *ICC 2019 - 2019 IEEE International Conference on Communications (ICC)*, 2019, pp. 1–6.

102. Y. Liu, M. Dong, K. Ota, and A. Liu, "Activetrust: Secure and trustable routing in wireless sensor networks," *IEEE Transactions on Information Forensics and Security*, vol. 11, pp. 2013–2027, 2016.

103. Z. Lu, Y. E. Sagduyu, and J. H. Li, "Securing the backpressure algorithm for wireless networks," *IEEE Transactions on Mobile Computing*, vol. 16, pp. 1136–1148, 2017.

104. N. C. Luong, T. T. Anh, H. T. T. Binh, D. Niyato, D. I. Kim, and Y. C. Liang, "Joint transaction transmission and channel selection in cognitive radio based blockchain networks: A deep reinforcement learning approach," in *Proceedings of the ICASSP 2019-2019 IEEE International Conference on Acoustics, Speech and Signal Processing (ICASSP)*, Brighton, UK, 2019, pp. 8409–8413.

105. T. Mahmood and et al., "An intelligent fault detection approach based on reinforcement learning system in wireless sensor network," *The Journal of Supercomputing*, vol. 78, no. 3, pp. 3646–3675, 2022.

106. P Manimala and R Senthamil, "A survey on leach-energy based routing protocol," *International Journal of Emerging Technology and Advanced Engineering (IJETAE)*, vol. 3, no. 12, pp. 657–660, 2013.

107. A. Manjeshwar and D. P. Agrawal, "Teen: A routing protocol for enhanced efficiency in wireless sensor networks," in *Proceedings 15th International Parallel and Distributed Processing Symposium. IPDPS 2001*, 2001, pp. 2009–2015.

108. N. Mazyavkina, S. Sviridov, S. Ivanov, and E. Burnaev, "Reinforcement learning for combinatorial optimization: A survey," *Comput. Oper. Res.*, vol. 134, p. 105 400, Oct. 2021.

109. C. M. Medaglia and A. Serbanati, "An overview of privacy and security issues in the internet of things," 2010.

110. K. P. Mhatre and U. P. Khot, "Energy efficient opportunistic routing with sleep scheduling in wireless sensor networks," *Wireless Pers. Commun.*, vol. 112, no. 2, pp. 1243–1263, Jan. 2020.

111. P. K. Mishra and S. K. Verma, "A survey on clustering in wireless sensor network," in *Proc. 11th Int. Conf. Comput., Commun. Netw. Technol. (ICCCNT)*, Kharagpur, India, Jul. 2020, pp. 1–5.

112. P. Mishra, S. Alaria, and P. Dangi, "Design and comparison of leach and improved centralized leach in wireless sensor network," *International Journal on Recent and Innovation Trends in Computing and Communication*, vol. 9, pp. 34–39, May 2021.

113. K. H. Mohammadani, K. A. Memon, I. Memon, N. N. Hussaini, and H. Fazal, "Preamble time-division multiple access fixed slot assignment protocol for secure mobile ad hoc networks," *International Journal of Distributed Sensor Networks*, vol. 16, no. 5, p. 1 550 147 720 921 624, 2020.

114. A. Moinet, B. Darties, and J.-L. Baril, "Blockchain based trust & authentication for decentralized sensor networks," 2017. arXiv: `1706.01730 [cs.CR]`.

115. M. Mounica, R. Vijayasaraswathi, and R. Vasavi, "Detecting sybil attack in wireless sensor networks using machine learning algorithms," *IOP Conference Series: Materials Science and Engineering*, vol. 1042, p. 012 029, Jan. 2021.

116. A. Mubarakali, "An efficient authentication scheme using blockchain technology for wireless sensor networks," *Wirel. Pers. Commun.*, vol. 127, pp. 255–269, 2021.

117. P. M. Mwangi, J. G. Ndia, and G. M. Muketha, "An extended k-means cluster head selection algorithm for efficient energy consumption in wireless sensor network," *International Journal of Network Security and its Applications*, vol. 15, no. 3, pp. 65–83, 2023.

118. A. Naderloo, S. A. Fatemi Aghda, and M. Mirfakhraei, "Fuzzy-based cluster routing in wireless sensor network," *Soft Computing*, vol. 27, no. 10, pp. 6151–6158, 2023, issn: 1433-7479.

119. S. Nageswararao and S. Chigarapalle, "Recommendations based qos trust aggregation and routing in mobile adhoc networks," *International Journal of Communication Networks and Information Security (IJCNIS)*, vol. 8, pp. 215–220, Dec. 2016.

120. C. Nakas, D. Kandris, and G. Visvardis, "Energy efficient routing in wireless sensor networks: A comprehensive survey," *Algorithms*, vol. 13, no. 3, p. 72, Mar. 2020.

121. J. Nam, U. S. R. K. Dhamodharan, and R. Vayanaperumal, "Detecting and preventing sybil attacks in wireless sensor networks using message authentication and passing method," *The Scientific World Journal*, vol. 2015, p. 841 267, 2015, issn: 2356-6140.

122. W. Neji, S. B. Othman, and H. Sakli, "T-leach: Threshold sensitive low energy adaptive clustering hierarchy for wireless sensor networks," in *2020 20th International Conference on Sciences and Techniques of Automatic Control and Computer Engineering (STA)*, 2020, pp. 336–342. doi: `10.1109/STA50679.2020.9329354`.

123. D. Nguyen, V. Dang, Q. Khanh, and T. Nguyen, "Intelligent blockchain-based edge computing via deep reinforcement learning: Solutions and challenges," *IEEE Network*, vol. 36, no. 6, pp. 12–19, 2022.

124. M. Nguyen, V.-C. Nguyen, and H. Tran, "A framework of deploying blockchain in wireless sensor networks," *EAI Endorsed Transactions on Industrial Networks and Intelligent Systems*, vol. 9, e3, Aug. 2022.

125. V.-C. Nguyen, M. Nguyen, T. B, T. Tran, and N. Duy, "Blockchain technology in wireless sensor network: Benefits and challenges," pp. 1–5, Sep. 2021.

126. K. Nicolas and Y. Wang, "A novel double spending attack countermeasure in blockchain," in *Proceedings of the 2019 IEEE 10th Annual Ubiquitous Computing, Electronics and Mobile Communication Conference (UEMCON)*, New York, NY, USA, 2019, pp. 383–388.

127. B. Omodunbi, O. Arulogun, and J. Emuoyibofarhe, "A review of energy conservation in wireless sensor networks," *Network and Complex Systems*, vol. 3, no. 5, p. 17, 2013.

128. J. Pan, J. Wang, A. Hester, I. Alqerm, Y. Liu, and Y. Zhao, "Edgechain: An edge-iot framework and prototype based on blockchain and smart contracts," *IEEE Internet of Things Journal*, vol. 6, pp. 4719–4732, 2018.

129. S. Panchal, G. Raval, and S. N. Pradhan, "Optimization of hierarchical routing protocol for wireless sensor networks with identical clustering," in *International Conference on Advances in Communication Network and Computing*, 2010.

130. L. W. Park, S. Lee, and H. Chang, "A sustainable home energy prosumer-chain methodology with energy tags over the blockchain," *Sustainability*, vol. 10, no. 3, 2018, issn: 2071-1050.

131. S. Pateria, B. Subagdja, A.-H. Tan, and C. Quek, "Hierarchical reinforcement learning: A comprehensive survey," *ACM Comput. Surveys*, vol. 54, no. 5, pp. 1–35, Jun. 2021.

132. D. Paulraj, L. R, T Jayasudha, M Ishwarya Niranjana, T Daniya, and F. Daniel Shadrach, "Blockchain-based wireless sensor network security through authentication and cluster head selection," in *2023 IEEE International Conference on Integrated Circuits and Communication Systems (ICICACS)*, 2023, pp. 1–5.

133. L. Pavithra *et al.*, "Blockchain based security analysis for fuzzy based systems," *IOP Conference Series: Materials Science and Engineering*, vol. 1084, p. 012 052, 2021.

134. A. T. D. Perera and P. Kamalaruban, "Applications of reinforcement learning in energy systems," *Renew. Sustain. Energy Rev.*, vol. 137, p. 110 618, Mar. 2021.

135. A. Primo, "A comparison of blockchain-based wireless sensor network protocols," in *2020 11th IEEE Annual Ubiquitous Computing, Electronics Mobile Communication Conference (UEMCON)*, 2020, pp. 0793–0799.

136. G. D. Putra, V. Dedeoglu, S. S. Kanhere, and R. Jurdak, "Trust-based blockchain authorization for iot," 2019. arXiv: `2104.00832 [cs.CR]`.

137. Y. Qiu, Y. Liu, X. Li, and J. Chen, "A novel location privacy-preserving approach based on blockchain," *Sensors*, vol. 20, p. 3519, 2020.

138. Y. Qu, G. Zheng, H. Wu, B. Ji, and H. Ma, "An energy-efficient routing protocol for reliable data transmission in wireless body area networks," *Sensors*, vol. 19, no. 19, 2019, issn: 1424-8220. [Online]. Available: `https://www.mdpi.com/1424-8220/19/19/4238`.

139. N. Qubbaj, A. A. Taleb, and W. Salameh, "Review on LEACH protocol," in *2020 11th International Conference on Information and Communication Systems (ICICS)*, IEEE, 2020, pp. 414–419.

140. Y. R, L Yepeng, S. Ji, A. K. Sangaiah, and J. Wang, "Incentive mechanism of data storage based on blockchain for wireless sensor networks," *Research on Efficient Data Forwarding in Vehicular Networks*, vol. 2018, Article ID 6874158, 2018.

141. A. Rahman, M. J. Islam, A. Montieri, M. K. Nasir, M. M. Reza, S. S. Band, A. Pescape, M. Hasan, M. Sookhak, and A. Mosavi, "Smartblock-sdn: An optimized blockchain-sdn framework for resource management in iot," *IEEE Access*, vol. 9, pp. 28 361–28 376, 2021.

142. G. Ramezan and C. Leung, "A blockchain-based contractual routing protocol for the internet of things using smart contracts," *Wireless Communications and Mobile Computing*, vol. 2018, p. 4 029 591, 2018, issn: 1530-8669.

143. S. Rani, X. Zheng, S. B. H. Shah, X. Ren, F. Li, L. Nawaf, C. Chakraborty, and M. Fayaz, "Mobile edge computing enabled efficient communication based on federated learning in internet of medical things," *Wireless Communications and Mobile Computing*, vol. 2021, p. 4 410 894, Oct. 27, 2021, issn: 1530-8669.

144. S. Rathore, J. H. Park, and H. Chang, "Deep learning and blockchain-empowered security framework for intelligent 5g-enabled iot," *IEEE Access*, vol. 9, pp. 90 075–90 083, 2021.

145. M. Revanesh and V. Sridhar, "A trusted distributed routing scheme for wireless sensor networks using blockchain and meta-heuristics-based deep learning technique," *Transactions on Emerging Telecommunications Technologies*, vol. 32, no. 4, e4193, 2021. doi: `10.1002/ett.4193`.

146. M. Saad, J. Spaulding, L. Njilla, C. Kamhoua, S. Shetty, D. Nyang, and D. Mohaisen, "Exploring the attack surface of blockchain: A comprehensive survey," *IEEE Communications Surveys Tutorials*, vol. PP, pp. 1–1, Mar. 2020.

147. Salam and M. Hossen, "Performance analysis on homogeneous LEACH and EAMMH protocols in wireless sensor network," *Wireless Personal Communications*, vol. 113, no. 1, pp. 189–222, 2020.

148. F. M. Salman, A. A. Mohammed, and A. F. Mutar, "Optimization of LEACH protocol for WSNs in terms of energy efficiency and network lifetime," *Journal of Cyber Security and Mobility*, vol. 12, no. 3, pp. 275–295, 2023.

149. S. Sangeetha and K. Prasad, "Reinforcement learning based blockchain and enhanced detection in iot networks," *ICTACT Journal on Communication Technology*, vol. Issue 14 Vol.-2, pp. 2952–2958, 2023.

150. S. Sayeed, H. Marco-Gisbert, and T. Caira, "Smart contract: Attacks and protections," *IEEE Access*, vol. 8, pp. 24 416–24 427, 2020.

151. S. A. Sert, E. Onur, and A. Yazici, "Security attacks and countermeasures in surveillance wireless sensor networks," in *Proceedings of the 2015 9th International Conference on Application of Information and Communication Technologies (AICT)*, Rostov-On-Don, Russia, 2015, pp. 201–205.

152. N. Shabbir and S. R. Hassan, "Routing protocols for wireless sensor networks (wsns)," in *Wireless Sensor Networks - Insights and Innovations*, InTech, 2017.

153. Z. Shahbazi and Y.-C. Byun, "Towards a secure thermal-energy aware routing protocol in wireless body area network based on blockchain technology," *Sensors*, vol. 20, no. 12, 2020, issn: 1424-8220.

154. A. Shahraki, A. Taherkordi, Ã˜ystein Haugen, and F. Eliassen, "Clustering objectives in wireless sensor networks: A survey and research direction analysis," *Computer Networks*, vol. 180, p. 107 376, 2020, issn: 1389-1286.

155. N. Sharma, B. M. Singh, and K. Singh, "Qos-based energy-efficient protocols for wireless sensor network," *Sustain. Comput., Informat. Syst.*, vol. 30, p. 100 425, Jun. 2021.

156. W. She, Q. Liu, Z. Tian, J.-S. Chen, B. Wang, and W. Liu, "Blockchain trust model for malicious node detection in wireless sensor networks," *IEEE Access*, vol. 7, pp. 38 947–38 956, 2019.

157. S. Shin and T. Kwon, "A lightweight three-factor authentication and key agreement scheme in wireless sensor networks for smart homes," *Sensors*, vol. 19, p. 2012, 2019.

158. N. Sindhwani and R. Vaid, "V LEACH: An energy efficient communication protocol for wsn," *CONFAB Journals*, 2013.

159. S. Singh and D. Subhash, "A review of trust and reputation models based on blockchain network," *International Journal of Control and Automation*, vol. 12, no. 4, pp. 207–217, 2019.

160. S. Singh and D. S. Chander, "A review of various trust based routing models in wireless sensor networks and iot," in *Proceedings of ICAML 2021 (PUP), Applications of AI and Machine Learning*, 2021, pp. 291–294.

161. S. Singh and D. S. Chander, "A novel blockchain-reinforcement learning framework for securing wireless sensor networks with energy efficiency," *International Journal on Recent and Innovation Trends in Computing and Communication*, vol. 11, no. 10, pp. 2256–2263, 2023, Scopus Indexed.

162. S. Singh and D. S. Chander, "Prevention of sybil attack on blockchain to ensure security of wireless sensor network," *International Journal of Systems and Applications in Engineering*, vol. 12, no. 8s, pp. 14–24, 2023, Scopus Indexed.

163. N. Storublevtcev, "Cryptography in blockchain," in Jun. 2019, pp. 495–508, isbn: 978-3-030-24295-4.

164. U. Suriya and R. Vayanaperumal, "Detecting and preventing sybil attacks in wireless sensor networks using message authentication and passing method," *TheScientificWorldJournal*, vol. 2015, p. 841 267, Jul. 2015.

165. G. Tamilselvan and K. Gandhimathi, "Network coding based energy-efficient leach protocol for wsn," *Journal of Applied Research and Technology*, vol. 17, no. 1, pp. 1–7, 2019.

166. Y. Teekaraman, D. K. Bangotra, Y. Singh, N. Kumar, P. Kumar Singh, and A. Ojeniyi, "Energy-efficient and secure opportunistic routing protocol for wsn: Performance analysis with nature-inspired algorithms and its application in biomedical applications," *BioMed Research International*, vol. 2022, p. 1 976 694, 2022, issn: 2314-6133.

167. H. T. Tran, C. V. Nguyen, and M. T. Nguyen, "A framework of deploying blockchain in wireless sensor networks," *EAI Endorsed Transactions on Industrial Networks and Intelligent Systems*, vol. 9, e3, 32 2022.

168. D. Tyagi, S. Ghosh, A. Rana, and V. Kansal, "A comparative analysis of potential factors and impacts that affect blockchain technology in software: Based applications," in *2020 9th International Conference System Modeling and Advancement in Research Trends (SMART)*, 2020, pp. 127–136.

169. A. Upadhyay, R. Kumar, and S. K. Tiwari, “Modified leach protocol for sensor network,” in *2015 International Conference on Futuristic Trends on Computational Analysis and Knowledge Management (ABLAZE)*, 2015, pp. 301–304.

170. R. Venkataraman, S. Moeller, B. Krishnamachari, and T. R. Rao, “Trust-based backpressure routing in wireless sensor networks,” *International Journal of Sensor Networks*, vol. 17, pp. 27–39, 2015.

171. G. Vishnupriya and R. Ramachandran, “A survey on tree-based energy efficient wireless sensor network,” in *Proc. Int. Conf. Commun. Signal Process. (ICCSP)*, Chennai, India, Jul. 2020, pp. 242–245.

172. Z. Wang, Y. Tian, and J. Zhu, “Data sharing and tracing scheme based on blockchain,” in *2018 8th International Conference on Logistics, Informatics and Service Sciences (LISS)*, 2018, pp. 1–6.

173. J. Xie, F. Yu, T. Huang, R. Xie, J. Liu, and Y. Liu, “A survey on the scalability of blockchain systems,” *IEEE Network*, vol. 33, pp. 166–173, 2019.

174. Z. Xie, R. Wu, M. Hu, and H. Tian, “Blockchain-enabled computing resource trading: A deep reinforcement learning approach,” in *2020 IEEE Wireless Communications and Networking Conference (WCNC)*, Seoul, Korea (South), 2020, pp. 1–8.

175. Z. Xiong, S. Feng, D. T. Niyato, P. Wang, and Z. Han, “Edge computing resource management and pricing for mobile blockchain,” *ArXiv*, vol. abs/1710.01567, 2017.

176. Y. Xu, G. Wang, J. Yang, J. Ren, Y. Zhang, and C. Zhang, “Towards secure network computing services for lightweight clients using blockchain,” *Wireless Communications and Mobile Computing*, vol. 2018, pp. 1–12, Nov. 2018.

177. J. Yang, S. He, Y. Xu, L. Chen, and J. Ren, “A trusted routing scheme using blockchain and reinforcement learning for wireless sensor networks,” *Sensors (Basel, Switzerland)*, vol. 19, no. 4, pp. 1–21, 2019. doi: 10.3390/s19040974.

178. J. Yang, S. He, Y. Xu, L. Chen, and J. Ren, “A trusted routing scheme using blockchain and reinforcement learning for wireless sensor networks,” *Sensors*, vol. 19, pp. 970–979, Feb. 2019.

179. M. Yang, T. Zhu, K. Liang, W. Zhou, and R. H. Deng, “A blockchain-based location privacy-preserving crowdsensing system,” *Future Generation Computer Systems*, vol. 94, pp. 408–418, 2019.

180. A. Yousaf, F. Ahmad, S. Hamid, and F. Khan, "Performance comparison of various leach protocols in wireless sensor networks," in *2019 IEEE 15th International Colloquium on Signal Processing & Its Applications, CSPA*, IEEE, 2019, pp. 108–113.

181. S. B. H. Youssef, S. Rekhis, and N. Boudriga, "A blockchain based secure iot solution for the dam surveillance," in *2019 IEEE Wireless Communications and Networking Conference (WCNC)*, 2019, pp. 1–6.

182. S. Zhai, Y. Yang, J. Li, C. Qiu, and J. Zhao, "Research on the application of cryptography on the blockchain," *Journal of Physics: Conference Series*, vol. 1168, p. 032 077, Feb. 2019.

183. G. Zhang, Y. Zhang, and Z. Chen, "Using trust to secure geographic and energy aware routing against multiple attacks," *PloS One*, vol. 8, no. 10, e77488, 2013.

184. Z. Zhao, G. Li, and M. Xu, "An improved algorithm based on LEACH routing protocol," in *2019 IEEE 19th International Conference on Communication Technology (ICCT)*, IEEE, 2019, pp. 1248–1251.

185. Z. Zheng, S. Xie, H.-N. Dai, X. Chen, and H. Wang, "Blockchain challenges and opportunities: A survey," *International Journal of Web and Grid Services*, vol. 14, p. 352, Oct. 2018.

186. M. H. Zurina, A. Arshad, S. Subramaniam, and R. Latip, "A survey of sybil attack countermeasures in iot-based wireless sensor networks," *PeerJ Computer Science*, vol. 7, Sep. 2021.

www.ingramcontent.com/pod-product-compliance
Lightning Source LLC
LaVergne TN
LVHW082342200926
848481LV00012B/3426